# LUNA PARK

# LUNA PARK

Short Plays and Monologues

## DONALD MARGULIES

THEATRE COMMUNICATIONS GROUP

NEW YORK

This publication is made possible in part with public funds from the New York State Council on the Arts, a State Agency.

TCG books are exclusively distributed to the book trade by Consortium Book Sales and Distribution, 1045 Westgate Dr., St. Paul, MN 55114.

LIBRARY OF CONGRESS CATALOGING-IN-PUBLICATION DATA
Margulies, Donald.
Luna Park : short plays and monologues / Donald Margulies.
p. cm.
ISBN 1-55936-206-5 (alk. paper)
I. Title.
PS3563.A653 L86    2001
812'.54—dc21        2001045685

Book design and typography by Lisa Govan
Cover design by Lisa Govan
Cover image (postcard of Luna Park at night) is copyright
© Lake County Museum/CORBIS
Author photo by Susan Johann

First edition, May 2002

# CONTENTS

NOCTURNE 1

LUNA PARK 7

MONOLOGUES 47

Louie 49
Anthony 53
Joey 57
Lola 63
Manny 67
I Don't Know What I'm Doing 73

SHORT PLAYS 79

Father and Son 81
Death in the Family 87
New Year's Eve and Kibbutz 93
Misadventure 109
Zimmer 115
Space 133
Women in Motion 141
L.A. 159
Pitching to the Star 173
July 7, 1994 203

*For my son, Miles*

# NOCTURNE

INSPIRED BY THE COLLAGES
OF MAX ERNST

*Nocturne* was commissioned by the Center Theatre Group of Los Angeles, Mark Taper Forum.

*Nocturne* was the curtain raiser for *Broken Sleep: Three Plays,* which also included *Broken Sleep* and *July 7, 1994*. Its world premiere took place at the Williamstown Theatre Festival on July 16, 1997. The director was Lisa Peterson. Original music was composed by Michael-John LaChiusa. The musical director was Georgia C. Stitt. The set design was by Kathleen Widomski, lighting was by Jeffrey Nellis and costumes and masks were by Linda Cho. The ensemble included Kate Burton, Tony Campisi, Divina Cook, Adriane Lenox, Paula Newsome and Cotter Smith. The Boy was played by Bryan Hughes.

*Night. A child's room. A brass bed. A full moon. A chair. A side table on which sits a basin and pitcher. An old-fashioned doll house is on the floor.*

*A title is projected and then fades out:*

## NOCTURNE

*A Boy in blue-and-white striped pajamas, his limbs in haphazard array (arm flung over his head, leg dangling off the bed), is fast asleep.*

*A gleaming, translucent orb rises out of his bed and hovers above him.*

*Title:*

## A WONDERFUL SURPRISE

*The Boy awakens to find the tantalizing object looming above him, sits up, then excitedly stands on the bed to try to take hold of it. He jumps up and down but the orb is elusive; it teases him, continually floating within the Boy's reach, then rising too high to be snatched. He leaps off the bed and follows it around the room. The Boy's hands are outstretched as the orb blows away in a whooshing wind.*

*Title:*

## ALL ALONE IN THE NIGHT

*The Boy looks around the room. A little spooked, he clutches his stuffed rabbit and sits in the chair.*

*The lights inside the doll house suddenly go on, casting shadows on the wall. The Boy turns his attention to the house and goes to it. He sits on the floor and plays, moving doll-like figures around the rooms.*

*Title:*

## THE SKY CRACKS OPEN

*There is a sudden crash of thunder and bursts of white lightning. The frightened Boy runs to the doorway and silently calls: "Mama! Daddy!" (We hear his recorded voice on tape.) He runs back to his bed and hides under his pillow.*

*Title:*

## I HEAR MONSTERS WHISPERING

*A Monster wearing a dark suit and lizard mask crawls out from under the bed. (These Monsters walk like humans, on two feet.) The Boy peers from behind his pillow watching the Lizard walk about, exploring the room. A second Monster, also in a suit and wearing an alligator mask, comes out holding an alligator-skin doctor's bag and joins him. Insidiously, they pick up the Boy's toys and inspect them as if they're foreign objects, consulting with one another in an eerie whisper, repeating: "Hush."*

*The Monsters put various playthings into the bag. The Boy is fearful at first, then curious, then incensed that the Monsters are taking his things without his permission. As the creatures are about to walk out the door, the Boy stands up in bed and shouts: "Hey!" The Monsters are startled; their green eyes light up when they see him.*

*Title:*

## UH OH!

*The Monsters take chase after the Boy, who runs around the room. Finally, the Boy dashes under the bed but the Lizard pulls him out by his foot. The Alligator brandishes a gleaming dagger and raises it to strike. The struggling Boy is about to scream but the Lizard covers his mouth. The Monsters' hushing continues.*

*Title:*

## A FLUTTERING OF WINGS

*A fluttering sound precedes the entrance of two Birds, both wearing long Victorian dresses with bustles. Their appearance reprieves the Boy. The Birds and the Monsters fight over the Boy, who is passed around from creature to creature. The squawking Birds succeed in driving the Monsters out the door. The Birds hold onto the Boy and prepare to take off with him in tow.*
    *Title:*

## I AM STOLEN!

*The terrified Boy opens his mouth to scream; he makes no sound but we hear a piercing, piteous wail (made by his Mother offstage) as he's whisked away by the Birds. The sound of wings flapping fades as he vanishes.*
    *The wailing continues as the Boy's barefoot, grief-stricken Mother, dressed in a nightgown, her long tresses flowing wildly, runs into the room gesturing dolefully with her hands, followed closely by the Boy's somber Father, also barefoot, wearing a smoking jacket and holding a lit candle.*
    *Title:*

## AN EMPTY BED

*The Mother sobs-sings a mournful melody as the Father tries to console her and get her to sit in the chair, while he sorrowfully caresses the lost Boy's blanket. But the Mother is too agitated to be still. She goes to the Father. He attempts to calm her but she makes harsh sounds of recrimination and pummels him with her fists. He takes hold of her hands, stopping her. She relents and lets him hold her in his arms. In the flickering candlelight, their lulling swaying becomes a tango of grief. The Boy appears briefly, high above the wall. He sees his parents dancing, then dips out of view.*

*There is a knock at the door. The Boy's parents stand together in trepidation.*
*Title:*

WHO IS AT THE DOOR?

*A Policeman in a long overcoat, wearing a handsome lion's head, appears in the doorway. The Mother gasps, puts her hand over her mouth. The Father wraps his arm around her.*

*In a moment, the Boy peers from behind the Policeman. The Mother opens her arms to embrace him. The grateful Father goes to shake the Policeman's hand. The Policeman leaves. The Boy enjoys an emotional reunion with his parents. They mime animated conversation.*
*Title:*

I TELL THEM ABOUT MY ADVENTURE
AND HOW I GOT TO RIDE IN A POLICE CAR

*But it's time to go back to sleep. The Mother puts him in bed and tucks him in. She hums a lullaby and kisses him. The Father kisses him, too, and goes. The Mother follows, glancing back at the Boy before she exits.*

*The Boy appears to have fallen back asleep, but in a moment, he sits up in bed, squirrels under his covers and emerges with—a translucent orb! Smiling in wonder, he holds it in his hands. The object begins to hover just above his hands.*
*Title:*

I HAVE MY PRIZE!

*The room is in darkness.*
*Title:*

THE END

# LUNA PARK

INSPIRED BY THE SHORT STORY
"IN DREAMS BEGIN RESPONSIBILITIES"
BY DELMORE SCHWARTZ

*In memory of my grandparents,*
*Rose and Jack Bender*

*Luna Park* was commissioned and produced by New York's Jewish Repertory Theatre (Ran Avni, Artistic Director) on February 6, 1982, as one-half of "Delmore: An Evening of Two One-Act Plays," which included *Shenandoah* by Delmore Schwartz. It was directed by Florence Stanley. The set design was by Ken Rothchild, lighting was by Carol B. Sealey, sound was by Andrew Howard and costumes were by Linda Vigdor. The cast was as follows:

| | |
|---|---|
| ROSE, USHER, VOICE OF GRANDMOTHER | Barbara Glenn Gordon |
| DELMORE, GRANDFATHER, MAN WALKING DOG, MAN FEEDING PIGEONS, MERRY-GO-ROUND OPERATOR, WAITER, PHOTOGRAPHER, FORTUNE TELLER | Willie Reale |
| YOUNG ROSE | Susan Merson |
| HARRY | David Wohl |

| | |
|---|---|
| ACTOR #1 (EARLY TWENTIES) | Delmore, Grandfather, Man Walking Dog, Man Feeding Pigeons, Merry-Go-Round Operator, Waiter, Photographer, Fortune Teller |
| ACTOR #2 (ABOUT TWENTY-NINE) | Harry |
| ACTRESS #1 (LATE FORTIES) | Rose, Usher, Voice of Grandmother |
| ACTRESS #2 (EARLY TWENTIES) | Young Rose |

TIME AND PLACE

The Prologue and Epilogue are set in the kitchen of the Schwartz apartment in New York City in December 1934.

The dream portion of the play begins in a movie theatre; the "film" which unfolds takes place in Brooklyn, primarily parts of Coney Island. The time is June 1909.

# PROLOGUE

*The time is December 1934.*

*Delmore sits at the kitchen table reading. His mother, Rose, stands at the sink washing dishes; she raises her voice to be heard over the running water. Her back is to him, his chair is turned away from her.*

*Long silence. Delmore yawns.*

ROSE: So you thinking it over what I said? *(Pause)* Thinking?

DELMORE *(Doesn't look up from his book)*: Uh-huh.

ROSE: I know I told you "anything." I don't mean *anything*. Believe me, it would be very nice if I could say "anything" and mean "*anything*" but this is the way with the world today. I'm very sorry. *(Scraping a dish into the trash)* How come you didn't touch your carrots?

DELMORE: I don't like carrots.

ROSE: Since when?

DELMORE: I've never liked carrots. I don't think I've ever really eaten carrots.

ROSE: Why didn't you tell me?

DELMORE: Why didn't you know?

*(Pause.)*

ROSE: I can't keep track of everything. I'm very sorry. I got a lot on my mind. *(A beat)* Should I save the carrots? *(She puts her hand in the garbage bag ready to retrieve them)* Huh?

DELMORE: If you want them, save them. I'm not going to eat them.

ROSE (*Thinks for a second*): Oh, I'll live without the carrots. I feel terrible. You know I don't like putting into the garbage what should go into your mouth. (*A beat, then to herself*) Damn the carrots. (*To Delmore, but she doesn't look at him*) Did you know that if you eat too many carrots your eyes turn yellow? Yes. Isn't that something? Who would believe something like that? (*Pause*) Next time tell me what you like instead of into the garbage. (*Pause*) I know what you could use and it makes a lot of sense: A scarf. How about a scarf of some kind? (*Delmore shrugs but she doesn't see him*) Answer me.

DELMORE: I said I don't care!!

ROSE: I didn't hear you, excuse me. (*Pause*) I'm sorry about the dinner. (*Pause*) Did you hear me?

DELMORE: Don't apologize.

ROSE: I didn't know how you feel about carrots, I'm sorry, it slipped my mind. I did what I could with the dinner.

DELMORE: It was a fine dinner.

ROSE: No. There's just so much I can do with what I got. Look, if your father had stayed with his wife and family . . . if your father was the responsible gentleman . . . hadn't thrown himself into a grave and taken every penny with him, there at least would have been a decent brisket on the table. And a cake! A birthday cake. With your name on it in sugar icing.

DELMORE: I don't care for cake.

ROSE: Who you kidding you don't care for cake. You love cake. A cake would've been perfect. A cake would've been wonderful. Twenty-one is a big deal. I tried to make you a slightly special supper. I'm sorry about the brisket. I asked for a reasonable-looking brisket. I told him, I can't pay you much but give me the most reasonable cut you got. Sure, Rose. So, what does he give me? Uch, fatty, terrible.

DELMORE: It was all right, Ma, it was all right.

ROSE: It was not all right. It was a terrible brisket. Fatty fatty. Sure, Rose, I believed him. I took his word. He's not an honest man but stupid Rose, I believed him. I should've known better than to trust that man but, oh, he has charm, a sense of humor. I feel so stupid I could spit. "You call that lean?" I says. "It's lean, it's lean," he says, "what do you want, bones?" Damn him! *(Long pause)* And he charges me an arm and a leg. For this terrible disgusting fatty unreasonable brisket. *Goniff.*

*(Delmore stands, heads for the doorway.)*

Where you going?

DELMORE: I, I think I'll read in bed.

ROSE: So you can burn up more electricity killing your eyes? Burning electricity costs money. You're not the son of Rockefeller no more I hate to tell you . . .

DELMORE *(Approaching the door)*: Good night.

ROSE: Stay till I finish up. So you'll read in here, why burn another bulb when you got this one going? Stay, sit, read.

*(A beat. Delmore relents.)*

Think over what you want for your birthday. Sit and think. You're smart, I'm sure you'll think of something. You got a big brain in there, what do you want? *(Delmore leans on the edge of the table)* What?

DELMORE: There's a book I want.

*(Pause. Rose stops what she's doing and looks at him.)*

ROSE: A book? *(Pause)* You're making a joke.

DELMORE: No I'm not.

ROSE: A book is very smart.

DELMORE: You asked me what I wanted!

ROSE: Yeah, but a book?! A book is just what you need. You must have twenty-*five* books in there! A book is not something you can wrap around your neck when the wind hits you like ice!

DELMORE: I don't want anything!

ROSE: But I want to *give* you something. This is no regular birthday . . . you can *vote* now. Isn't that wonderful? You can vote for the President of the United States! *(As she speaks, Delmore notices a tear in her sweater. A beat)* What.

DELMORE *(Surprised)*: Your sweater is ripped.

ROSE *(Tries to hide it)*: It's nothing.

DELMORE: Why haven't you sewn it?

ROSE: Never mind.

DELMORE: Why don't you mend it? It's in the seam . . .

ROSE: I'll live with it. Don't worry about it. *(She takes off the sweater, throws it over a chair)*

DELMORE: The slightest tear, the smallest pull of a thread, and you'd be stitching it right up. This is so unlike you.

ROSE *(Welling up with tears; yells)*: This *isn't* unlike me! This *is* me! *(She cries)* This is *me* . . .

*(Pause. Delmore watches her, uncertain of what to do.)*

DELMORE: I'll get your basket so you can fix it. *(He starts to go)*

ROSE *(Composing herself)*: No. Forget about it. The sweater is shot. It kept me warm enough years. It's shot, it's not worth it, don't worry about it, it's not your problem. *(She blows her nose)* There's just so much I can do with what I got. I'm sorry if you don't like it.

DELMORE: I'm not criticizing you.

ROSE *(Again, in tears)*: Yes you are! Look how you look at me! You look at me like I got a disease! Stop it!

DELMORE *(Turns away from her)*: I'm just trying to understand.

ROSE: What, Professor? What don't you understand?

DELMORE: I don't know how we got here, Ma. How'd this happen?

ROSE: This isn't what I had in mind. Believe me. I had other plans. *(She cries. Delmore tries to comfort her but cannot)* Leave me now. Leave me. Go, sleep. When you wake up, you'll be twenty-one. Go. *(Delmore hesitates, then exits. Pause, then to herself)* If only there was a cake . . .

*(Fade out.*

*Lights up. Delmore in his bedroom. He goes to a phono-graph and turns on a record. Rose's faint sobs meld into a scratchy recording of a Haydn string quartet.*

*Delmore paces the room as he undresses and gets into his pajamas. He examines himself in a mirror for a while. Soon he settles into bed with a book. He dozes off.*

*A shift in the lighting indicates passage of time. Delmore is in a deep sleep. We hear the needle of the phonograph skip-ping and the amplified sound of heavy restful breathing.*

*Fade out. The sounds continue in the darkness.)*

## SCENE ONE

*As a flashlight pierces the darkness, there is a surge of organ music, the kind played in movie palaces in the early part of the century.*

*The stage is clear except for a movie theatre seat which is situ-ated at rear center, facing the audience.*

*The flashlight is held by an Usher, who enters showing Delmore to his seat. The Usher is played by Rose. She wears the sweater Rose wore in the Prologue. Delmore is barefoot and wearing his pajamas. The Usher speaks in an exaggerated sibilant whisper.*

USHER: Shhh . . . You just made it. Sit still. Don't make a sound.

*(The sound of a movie projector is heard. A beam of flicker-ing light is shone on the audience from behind Delmore.)*

It's starting.

*(Young Rose enters from stage right and faces the audience.)*

Look what a beauty your mother was . . . *(The Usher begins to exit stage right. Harry enters, left, and faces the audience)* And there *he* is . . . *(Harry jingles the change in his pocket)* Yeah, that's him . . . *(The Usher stands near Young Rose. She takes off her sweater; to Delmore)* It's June 12, 1909. A Sunday. A beautiful day in Brooklyn. A chill is in the air. *(The Usher drapes the sweater over Young Rose's shoulders)* Now shush and shut up and watch the movie.

*(The Usher exits. The sound of the projector becomes louder, the flickering lights brighter. In a beat, Delmore runs offstage.*
   *Door chimes.*
   *Pause.*
   *Door chimes again. Rose is now heard as the offstage voice of her own mother, Delmore's Grandmother.)*

GRANDMOTHER'S VOICE: Just a second . . . Joseph, get the door. *(Door chimes again)* Joseph! Please! I'm washing dishes . . .

GRANDFATHER'S VOICE *(Spoken by Delmore)*: Just a second!

*(Lights up.*
   *Harry waits to be admitted to the home of Delmore's grandparents. Harry fixes his necktie and takes a deep breath.*
   *In a beat, Delmore hurriedly enters as his own Grandfather. He wipes his mouth with a napkin, clears his throat, then opens the front door.)*

GRANDFATHER: Oh! Mr. Schwartz . . . *(Grandfather wipes his hands thoroughly with his napkin)*

HARRY: Mr. Nathanson . . . you're eating. *(Grandfather takes Harry's hand, shakes it)*

GRANDFATHER: No, Mr. Schwartz, I'm shaking your hand. Come in.

HARRY *(Fumbling with his watch)*: I thought I planned it perfect. I told Rose "one." Please, eat, make believe I'm not here.

GRANDMOTHER'S VOICE: Joseph, who is it?

GRANDFATHER *(Calls to her)*: It's Harry Schwartz.

HARRY *(Calls)*: Hello, Mrs. Nathanson.

GRANDMOTHER'S VOICE: Oh, hello, Mr. Schwartz. It's one o'clock already?

HARRY AND GRANDFATHER: No, no . . .

GRANDFATHER: He's a couple minutes early.

HARRY: I'm a little early.

GRANDMOTHER'S VOICE: You're a little bit early I think.

HARRY: Yes. So it seems.

GRANDFATHER: Relax, Mr. Schwartz.

HARRY: Please, Mr. Nathanson, go eat.

GRANDFATHER: I ate, relax. Are you uncomfortable or something, Mr. Schwartz?

HARRY: No . . .

GRANDMOTHER'S VOICE: Is he uncomfortable or something?

HARRY *(Calls)*: No.

GRANDMOTHER'S VOICE: Tell him to sit down.

GRANDFATHER: Sit down, Mr. Schwartz.

*(Harry and Grandfather sit.)*

HARRY: Please, I didn't mean to interrupt your meal . . .

GRANDFATHER: You didn't interrupt.

GRANDMOTHER'S VOICE: Is he hungry?

HARRY: No . . .

GRANDFATHER: He says no.

GRANDMOTHER'S VOICE: Mr. Schwartz, feel like nibbling on a little brisket?

HARRY: No, thank you . . .

GRANDMOTHER'S VOICE: It's a wonderful lean brisket.

HARRY: So, where *is* Rose?

GRANDFATHER: Upstairs. Staring in the mirror.

HARRY: Oh, I see.

*(Harry and Grandfather share a knowing laugh.)*

GRANDFATHER: You know how Rose is, making sure everything is just so.

HARRY: Yes . . . *(Pause)*

GRANDFATHER: So, Mr. Schwartz . . . Tell me: how was traveling from New York?

HARRY: Oh, I had an exceptionally nice walk.

GRANDFATHER: You *walked*, Mr. Schwartz?

GRANDMOTHER'S VOICE: What, Joseph?

GRANDFATHER *(Calls)*: Mr. Schwartz walked, he says.

GRANDMOTHER'S VOICE: He walked?! Oh my God! All the way to Brooklyn?

HARRY: Yes . . .

GRANDMOTHER'S VOICE: That's some distance!

HARRY: Yes . . .

GRANDMOTHER'S VOICE: Across the bridge and everything?

HARRY: Yes . . .

GRANDMOTHER'S VOICE: My God!

HARRY: I love to walk. Walking is exceptional exercise.

GRANDMOTHER'S VOICE: What an ambitious young man . . .

GRANDFATHER: Yes, what an ambitious young man!

HARRY: And what an exceptional day for a walk!

GRANDFATHER: Perfect.

HARRY: Yes.

GRANDFATHER: A perfect day for a walk. A perfect day all around.

HARRY: Yes. And what a sight from the bridge: the Statue of Liberty, her lantern high in the blue, blue sky, the stars and stripes blowing in the breeze!

*(Harry and Grandfather sigh reverently.)*

GRANDMOTHER'S VOICE: What he say, Joseph?

GRANDFATHER: The Statue of Liberty! The stars and stripes!

*(We hear Grandmother also sigh.)*

GRANDMOTHER'S VOICE: You picked a beautiful day for a walk, Mr. Schwartz.

18

HARRY: Walking lets me clear my head, gives me a chance to smoke some expensive cigars.

GRANDMOTHER'S VOICE: You smoke cigars, Mr. Schwartz?

HARRY: Yes.

GRANDMOTHER'S VOICE: And why not?! If you enjoy it . . .

GRANDFATHER: Would you like a cigar, Mr. Schwartz?

GRANDMOTHER'S VOICE: Joseph, if you're going to start with the cigar smoke, open the window.

HARRY: Would *you* like a cigar, Mr. Nathanson? *(Harry takes two cigars from the inside pocket of his jacket)*

GRANDFATHER *(Extends a cigar to Harry)*: No, take one of mine, young man.

HARRY: These cigars are very, very expensive, Mr. Nathanson, and very, very high quality. Please take one.

GRANDFATHER: My cigar is a fine cigar, Mr. Schwartz.

HARRY: Yes, but mine are from Havana, Cuba.

*(A beat. Grandfather hesitates, then takes Harry's cigar. They sit silently for a little while as they light their cigars.)*

GRANDFATHER: So . . . how's business, Mr. Schwartz?

HARRY: You're asking the right person about business.

GRANDFATHER: Oh, yes?

*(Harry sits forward in his chair and speaks confidentially to Grandfather:)*

HARRY: Just between you and me, Mr. Nathanson, I'll let you in on a little secret: business is doing very nice . . . *(Grasps Grandfather's hand for emphasis) Very* nice.

GRANDFATHER: Good for you.

HARRY: And *this* week, Mr. Nathanson, I'm not embarrassed to tell you . . . This week business was exceptional.

GRANDFATHER: Good.

HARRY: Better than ever.

GRANDFATHER: *Mazel tov.*

HARRY: Better even than *last* week.

GRANDFATHER: Good!

HARRY: And last week I thought things couldn't be better.

*(During this last line, Young Rose enters. She is wearing the cardigan that was draped over her shoulders earlier by the elder Rose. Harry is made momentarily uneasy by her presence, uncertain whether to greet her or continue his conversation with Grandfather. Young Rose stands timidly, waiting to be acknowledged.)*

But *this* week, Mr. Nathanson, through the roof!

*(Harry laughs. Grandfather joins him briefly. Young Rose smiles broadly but doesn't understand the context of the laughter. When the joke dies down, there is an uncomfortable pause. Then Harry stands clumsily and greets her.)*

Hello.

YOUNG ROSE *(Hereafter referred to as Rose)*: Hello. *(Pause)*

HARRY: Hello, Rose.

ROSE: Hello, Harry.

*(Grandfather begins to cough from the cigar smoke. To Grandfather:)*

Are you all right?

*(Grandfather nods his head while choking.)*

GRANDMOTHER'S VOICE: Joseph, are you coughing? I told you open the window!

*(Pause. Grandfather's seizure stops.)*

HARRY: So, Rose, are you ready for Coney Island?

GRANDFATHER: Coney Island? Is that where you're taking Rose, Mr. Schwartz?

HARRY: Yes.

GRANDFATHER *(Joking)*: I'd love to go to Coney Island. What if I came along?

*(Harry and Rose laugh briefly. Silence.)*

HARRY *(To Rose)*: Ready?

ROSE. Yes, Harry.

HARRY *(Refers to her sweater)*: You don't need that.

ROSE: I don't?

HARRY: It's a beautiful day.

ROSE: But, still, I might get cold.

HARRY: Nah . . .

ROSE: There's a chill in the air I think.

HARRY: No, this is a day you just want to breathe, you don't want clothing to get in the way between you and the air.

ROSE: But it might get chilly.

HARRY: It's like summer, Rose, I promise you. The sun is shining and hot.

GRANDFATHER: Rose, Mr. Schwartz says you can do without the sweater.

*(Rose looks at Grandfather, then at Harry. In a beat, she takes the sweater off her shoulders and holds it.)*

HARRY: What an exceptional dress you have on, Rose.

ROSE: Thank you.

HARRY: Look at you! Why would you want to cover up such a beautiful dress?

*(Pause. Rose folds the sweater over the back of a chair.)*

*(Looking at Rose)* Do you want to know something, Mr. Nathanson?

21

GRANDFATHER: What?

HARRY: Your daughter and my business have something in common.

GRANDFATHER: Oh, yes?

HARRY *(Still looking at Rose)*: Yes. They're both looking extremely exceptional.

*(Rose giggles. Silence.*

*Tableau: Harry is facing Rose, who has turned away in embarrassment. Grandfather strokes his chin as he scrutinizes the couple.*

*Lights begin to fade out except for spots on the faces of Rose, Harry and Grandfather.*

*Fade out. Sound of rustling leaves is heard in the darkness.)*


SCENE TWO


*A tree-lined street in Brooklyn. Ocean Parkway.*

*Rose and Harry enter from the right and slowly stroll across the stage.*

*Delmore, disguised as a man walking a dog, enters from the left. He eavesdrops on Rose and Harry in mid-conversation.*

ROSE: What was that word?

HARRY: Exceptional?

ROSE: Yes. Exceptional. That's what this girl is. She got everything going for her. She's exceptional pretty, got a good head on her shoulders, good taste in clothes, and the kind of smile . . . her face brightens everybody's day!

HARRY: Ugh.

ROSE: On the outside she looks happy, but on the inside she's not really happy.

HARRY: Of course.

ROSE: All she does is hope that the man of her dreams will come along.

HARRY: Naturally.

ROSE: And then she meets George.

HARRY: Ah! George!

ROSE: She wants to marry George and have children and live in a lovely place, not too big, not too small.

HARRY: How long is this book? *(A beat. They stop walking. Rose is embarrassed)* So go on. *(Pause)* Tell me: what happens to this exceptional girl and what'shisname?

ROSE: George.

HARRY: George.

ROSE: Like George Washington. *(Says "Vashington")*

HARRY: Well? . . .

ROSE: To her, George is the most wonderful man in the world. But George practically doesn't know she's alive. He always has an eye on the girls (if you know what I mean), but she decides to wait until he comes to his senses and see that *she* is the only woman who will ever really love him.

HARRY *(Feigned concern)*: Hmm . . .

ROSE: And then they see each other at the square dance. *(She says "skvair dence")*

HARRY: Where?

ROSE: Square dance? *(She suggests the dance with her hands)*

HARRY *(Not really understanding)*: Oh.

*(A beat. He takes hold of Rose and gently dances with her, to her surprise.)*

And George dances with her . . . and then what?

ROSE *(Through giggles, still dancing)*: George dances with her . . . and the music plays . . . and he spins her around . . .

HARRY: Like this? *(Spins her around quickly)*

ROSE *(Caught up in the excitement)*: Yes! And they look into each other's eyes . . .

*(Suddenly, Harry stops dancing. He has stepped in droppings left by Delmore's "dog." He angrily looks at Delmore,*

*who stands nearby; Delmore shrugs an apology. Harry scrapes his shoe on the sidewalk while Rose looks on, bemused but disappointed that the dance ended so abruptly. Rose giggles nervously. Pause. Harry continues to scrape his shoe against the pavement.)*

You should read the way the writer writes it. It made me cry. He did some job, that writer. What a way with words.

HARRY: So George and this girl, they live happily ever after, huh?

ROSE: Well, no.

HARRY: No?

ROSE: Well, they fall in love and get married and for a little while they're happy. And they have children. And then they trick each other.

HARRY: Trick?

ROSE: Fool. They fool each other. They make things up. They don't tell the truth. They trick each other.

HARRY: Lies.

ROSE: Yes. Little lies. Little lies that get bigger and bigger, until she can't look at George in the eye no more.

*(They briefly make eye contact but turn away from one another. A depressed silence.)*

HARRY: What are you so sad about? It's just a silly book!

ROSE: Do you think so?

HARRY: I don't know what good books are if they make people sad. We're going to Coney Island! I promise you'll forget all about George and this silly girl . . .

ROSE: A walk on the boardwalk would be nice . . .

HARRY: And Luna Park! What about Luna Park!?

ROSE: No . . .

HARRY: I'll take you there, Rose . . .

ROSE: Not today, thank you. Not today Luna Park. Not that class of people and all that crazy noise and light. No, some other time Luna Park.

HARRY: Whatever you want, Rose. I promise. Forget about that
sad silly book . . . we're going to Coney Island!

*(Rose and Harry resume walking across the stage.*
*Tableau: they're frozen in mid-step. Rose looks at Harry,*
*whose expression is that of uncertainty. Delmore, as the man*
*walking a dog, glances over his shoulder at them.*
*Lights fade except for three lingering spots on their faces.*
*Fade out. The sound of the ocean is heard in the darkness.)*


SCENE THREE

*On the boardwalk in Coney Island.*
*Rose and Harry are leaning on the railing watching the ocean.*
*Delmore stands nearby, at another segment of railing, disguised*
*in unkempt clothing as a man tossing crumbs to pigeons.*

HARRY: Ah! Take a whiff of that sea air!
ROSE: Yes.
HARRY: Smell it. Take a deep breath and smell it.
ROSE *(Inhales; then)*: Yes.
HARRY: No, really smell it. Feel it fill your head.

*(He instructs her how to inhale. She laughs, then he does, too.*
*Long silence.)*

This is the best air you could breathe.
ROSE: It's very good for you.
HARRY: What?
ROSE: It's good for you, this air.
HARRY: The best. It's good for the lungs and the whole inter-
nal system. *(Pause)* I believe in health.
ROSE: Health is the most important thing, yes. Even more than
having money. All I want is health.

HARRY: That's all.

ROSE *(After a beat)*: And money.

*(They laugh. Pause.)*

HARRY: I believe in things that are good for you. *(Takes a cigar from his inside pocket and lights it)* Some people don't know what good is.

ROSE: Fruit for instance.

HARRY: Yes, fruit. Also, vegetables. *(He says "veg-e-tables")*

ROSE: Spinach . . .

HARRY: I don't care for spinach.

ROSE: Oh. Peas, string beans . . .

HARRY: Carrots . . .

ROSE: Carrots I like very much. I could eat carrots every day.

HARRY: Don't eat too many carrots.

ROSE: Why?

HARRY: Too much is no good for you.

ROSE: Why?

HARRY: It does something to your eyes.

ROSE: My *eyes?*

HARRY: Too many carrots make your eyes turn yellow.

ROSE: You're making a joke . . .

HARRY: No, I'm telling the truth: your eyes will turn yellow if you eat too many carrots.

ROSE: You're trying to fool me . . .

HARRY: Why would I fool you?

ROSE: I think you're making a joke.

HARRY: Young lady, I am not making a joke. I'm telling you a scientific fact: too many carrots in your system and your eyes will turn yellow.

ROSE: But my eyes are practically black, how can they go from black to yellow?

HARRY *(His patience flagging)*: The white part *around* your eyes . . .

ROSE: Oh. *(Pause)* Still, I don't believe you.

HARRY: Why would I lie about something like this?

ROSE: To fool me.

HARRY: No, I wouldn't do that.

ROSE: Well, I still think this business about carrots is a trick. You want me to believe it but I can't.

HARRY: Then believe what you wish.

*(A disturbed silence. They lean on the railing and look at the ocean, although they're preoccupied. Delmore, who has eavesdropped on them all along, continues to toss crumbs to pigeons.)*

*(Trying to lighten things up)* Peanuts?

ROSE: What?

HARRY: Peanuts?

ROSE *(A beat)*: I don't understand . . .

HARRY *(Hiding his exasperation)*: Would you like me to get you some peanuts? *(A beat)* Peanuts are good for you. You can eat all you want, your eyes won't change color.

ROSE *(Charmed)*: All right.

HARRY: I'll be right back.

*(Rose nods. Harry exits. Rose leans on the railing and looks at the ocean impassively.*

*The weather begins to change; the lighting dims and sounds of the wind and waves grow intense. Rose crosses her arms and holds herself to keep warm. She looks around for Harry but doesn't see him.)*

DELMORE *(As the man feeding pigeons)*: The tide is changing.

ROSE *(Realizes he's talking to her)*: What?

DELMORE: The tide. Do you hear it? It's getting rougher. *(A beat. Rose doesn't know what to make of him)* Do you see how the waves somersault? Roll and crack, roll and crack . . . Listen to it.

*(Rose has begun to chatter from the cold. She looks for Harry again.)*

Look at the ocean!

ROSE *(Uncomfortably)*: Very nice.

DELMORE *(Amused by her casual response)*: Very nice? *(A beat. He notices she's shivering)* Your teeth are chattering . . .

ROSE: Please go away.

DELMORE: Don't you have a sweater to put on?

*(Harry enters with a bag of peanuts.)*

ROSE: Harry . . . *(Rose giggles nervously and whispers)* Harry, there's a crazy man over there . . . *(Harry looks at Delmore, then protectively leads Rose a few feet away)*

DELMORE: I was just pointing out the beauty of the ocean . . .

HARRY: Never mind, mister.

DELMORE: . . . Look at it! It's right in front of your eyes!

ROSE *(Quietly, to Harry)*: Harry, please, can we go . . . ?

HARRY: We were here first, we're not going anywhere.

ROSE *(Shivering)*: Please . . .

HARRY: We had this spot first.

ROSE: But the wind is like ice.

DELMORE: The tide is changing.

HARRY: It's an exceptional day, enjoy it.

DELMORE: She's freezing.

HARRY *(The fight escalates)*: That's none of your business, mister.

DELMORE: How can you let her stand there shivering?

ROSE: Harry, please . . .

HARRY *(Overlapping)*: Mister, butt out!

DELMORE: Give her your jacket. Don't let her stand there shaking . . .

HARRY: Don't tell me what to do . . .

DELMORE: You *look* like a responsible gentleman . . .

*(Harry is about to hit him. Rose restrains him.)*

ROSE: Harry, please, I don't want to stand here no more.

HARRY: It's a matter of principle, Rose.

ROSE: But let's go inside someplace.

DELMORE: Give her your jacket at least.

HARRY: Mister . . .

ROSE: Harry . . .

HARRY *(Begins to take off his jacket)*: Here.

ROSE: No.

HARRY: Put it on. You won't be cold.

ROSE: I don't want it.

HARRY: You said you were cold.

ROSE: I don't want your jacket. If you had let me take my sweater, everything would be fine.

HARRY: Oh, so this is *my* fault? You didn't have to listen to me . . .

ROSE: But you promised me I wouldn't need it!

HARRY: I'm very sorry! I'm not the *Farmer's Almanac*!

DELMORE: Don't be a fool, take her inside.

*(Harry is enraged again and points his finger pugnaciously at Delmore.)*

ROSE: Harry, let's go . . .

HARRY *(Looking at Delmore)*: Of course, Rose. *(He takes her arm and begins to lead her off)* Whatever you like.

*(Harry crumples the bag of peanuts and tosses it behind him. Delmore picks up the bag and tosses peanuts to the birds.*

*Tableau: Rose and Harry in mid-step. Only their backs are visible [their exit is not quite complete] but Harry has turned his head for a final look at Delmore.*

*Lights begin to fade except for three spots on their faces.*

*Fade out. A sudden burst of calliope music is heard in the darkness.)*

SCENE FOUR

*On a merry-go-round.*

*Rose and Harry move in such a way as to suggest the rotation of a carousel. Perhaps they're holding wooden horses' heads.*

*Delmore, disguised as the merry-go-round operator is tending to the rings which the riders try to grasp.*

*The riders' movement becomes faster, the music louder, and their moods more exultant.*

*Harry laughs. Rose giggles uncontrollably. They make repeated grabs for rings; Delmore fixes it so that Harry consistently gets them and Rose always misses.*

*The music accelerates until it ends abruptly in a sour screech. Silence.*

*Blackout. The sound of the ocean is heard in the darkness.*

SCENE FIVE

*A restaurant on the boardwalk.*

*Rose and Harry are seated at a table finishing dinner.*

*Sound of distant violin.*

HARRY: So . . . ?
ROSE: Wonderful.
HARRY: Yes?
ROSE: Exceptional.
HARRY: What did I tell you? Didn't I promise you?
ROSE: Yes.
HARRY: I didn't lie when I said this is the best restaurant in
      Coney Island.
ROSE: No.
HARRY: This is the best.
ROSE: So you said. *(A beat)* Thank you.

HARRY: Don't thank me. It's my pleasure. It gives me pleasure to take you to the best restaurant.

ROSE *(Shyly)*: Thank you.

HARRY: Don't thank me. *(A beat)* You should've ordered the lobster.

*(Delmore, disguised as a waiter, enters during above and stands by his station.)*

ROSE: But I liked the fish . . .

HARRY *(Overlapping)*: I saw your face when you saw the price. You don't have to be shy with me, Rose. As long as you're with Harry Schwartz, you can have a-ny-thing you want. *(A short but pregnant pause)* Rose.

ROSE: Yes, Harry?

HARRY: Rose . . .

*(Delmore breaks the tense moment by coming between them with a pitcher of water. He refills their glasses.)*

DELMORE: Would you like to see dessert menus?

*(Rose shakes her head no to Harry. A beat)*

HARRY *(To Delmore)*: Yes. Yes, please. *(To Rose)* Their desserts are outta this world.

*(Delmore hands a menu to Rose; she refuses it. Harry takes his.)*

Have something.

ROSE: I don't want nothing.

DELMORE: Today's special dessert is chocolate layer cake.

HARRY *(For Rose's benefit)*: That sounds good.

DELMORE: It's our specialty.

HARRY *(To Rose)*: It's their specialty.

ROSE *(Growing uncomfortable)*: Don't worry about me.

HARRY *(Looking over the menu)*: How about orange sherbet?
ROSE: No.
HARRY *(To Delmore)*: A very particular young lady.

*(Delmore chuckles briefly with Harry; Rose is annoyed and embarrassed.)*

ROSE: Okay I'll have the sherbet.
HARRY: Good.
DELMORE *(To Rose)*: Are you sure you want the sherbet? There isn't much to it.
ROSE: Yes . . .
DELMORE: It's not much of a portion. It's sweet, but over very quickly. Have the chocolate layer cake.
ROSE: No. I'll have the sherbet.
DELMORE: The chocolate layer cake is rich and delicious. And the portion is impressive.
ROSE: No. The sherbet, please. *(A beat)*
DELMORE: All right.
HARRY: Strawberry cheesecake. *(Harry closes the menu, returns it to Delmore)*
DELMORE *(Repeats to himself)*: Strawberry cheesecake. Coffee? *(Harry looks to Rose)*
ROSE *(To Harry)*: Tea.
HARRY *(To Delmore)*: Two teas, please. *(Delmore nods, begins to exit. Harry calls after him)* In a glass.

*(Delmore exits. Pause.)*

ROSE: Finish what you were saying.
HARRY: Saying?
ROSE: Before. You said to me, as long as I'm with Harry Schwartz . . .
HARRY *(A beat)*: Oh. Yes. *(Pause)* You know, Rose, I go for the finer things in life . . .
ROSE: I do, too, Harry.

HARRY: An expensive cigar at my fingertips, nice material on
    my back . . .
ROSE: Yes . . .
HARRY: Good food in my stomach . . .
ROSE: Yes . . .

*(Romantic music slowly begins to build in intensity.)*

HARRY: A comfortable place to live . . .
ROSE: . . . not too big, not too small . . .
HARRY: . . . that's got heat when it's snowing, and maybe a bun-
    galow by the ocean where you can cool off when every-
    body else sweats . . .
ROSE *(An excited giggle)*: Yes . . .
HARRY: I earned these things, Rose. I *earned* them.
ROSE: And you should be proud of yourself.
HARRY: I *am* proud of myself. Why shouldn't I be proud of
    myself? I've come a long way since I got off the boat: a
    thirteen-year-old kid with big eyes and skinny ribs and
    holes in his pockets. *(Delmore enters carrying a tray, sets it
    down)* America's been good to me, Rose, and now I think
    it's time to settle down . . .

*(The music, which had begun to surge, stops abruptly when
Delmore interrupts; he stands between them with the dessert
plates in his hands: plain cheesecake and chocolate layer cake.)*

DELMORE *(Crassly)*: Okay, who's got the chocolate layer cake?
HARRY *(A beat)*: Neither of us.
DELMORE: Are you sure?
HARRY *(Losing patience)*: I ordered the *straw*berry cheesecake
    and the young lady is having the sherbet.
DELMORE: I was mistaken.
HARRY: Yes.
DELMORE *(To Rose)*: Would you like it now that I've brought it?
HARRY: No she would not. And I wanted *straw*berry cheesecake.

DELMORE: Terribly sorry.

*(Delmore exits. Pause.)*

ROSE: Go on, Harry.
HARRY: What was I saying?
ROSE: You were talking about settling down?
HARRY: Oh, yes. Settling down.

*(The romantic music begins to build once more.)*

You know, Rose, in the real estate game you get to see a lot of people settle down. That definitely has its rewards (in more ways than one, if you know what I mean). It's nice to see people planting roots and it's also nice earning a very handsome living. But, lately, it does something to me, Rose . . . it does something inside of me seeing these men (my age and even younger) with their pretty wives and children . . .
ROSE: Children?
HARRY: . . . building homes for themselves on land *I* sold them. It does something to me. I want that, too. After all, I'm twenty-nine years old, almost thirty, and it's time already.

*(Delmore reenters with the dessert tray as Harry speaks and interrupts him. Again, the music stops when Delmore intrudes.)*

DELMORE: I'm sorry but we're out of strawberry cheesecake. Would you like the plain?
HARRY *(Enraged)*: Will you leave us alone please?!
DELMORE: I'm just trying to do my job, sir.
HARRY: Well, not now.
DELMORE: Do you or don't you want the cheesecake without the strawberries?
HARRY: I want you to go away.

*(Delmore sets down the sherbet, the plain cheesecake and two glasses of tea.)*

DELMORE: Enjoy.

*(Delmore steps away from them but doesn't exit. He stands at his station folding napkins and shining silverware.)*

HARRY *(To Rose)*: My God, some nerve . . .
ROSE *(Anxiously)*: Harry, finish what you were saying . . .
HARRY *(Loud enough for Delmore to hear)*: I should report him to the head waiter . . .
ROSE: Harry, please . . . finish . . .
HARRY *(A beat)*: What I'm saying is . . .

*(The music begins to build again as he speaks.)*

I can promise you a comfortable life, Rose. You'll never have to worry about anything. I'll take care of you always, Rose, I'll make sure your pretty face stays smiling always.
ROSE: You think I'm pretty, Harry?
HARRY: Yes. Very pretty.
ROSE *(Softly, pleased)*: Oh. Good.
HARRY: And, Rose, I'll be good to you. You'll never be cold or hungry. I'll give you anything you want.
ROSE: Children, Harry?

*(Delmore drops some silverware and bends down to pick them up.)*

HARRY *(Glances at Delmore; a beat)*: If that's what you want . . . *(Rose nods)* So then, Rose . . . *(Nervously)* What do you think? *(He sighs)* Will you be my wife?

*(Delmore stands over the fallen silverware, frozen and help-less as he watches this momentous event. The music continues.)*

ROSE *(Welling up with tears)*: Yes! Yes. Harry, I will! It would make me so happy to be your wife!

DELMORE *(With dread, to himself)*: Oh, no . . .

ROSE *(Excited, tearful)*: I had a feeling you were going to ask me today.

HARRY: You did?

ROSE: I was *hoping* you would, from the first time I saw you. "What a respectable gentleman," I thought to myself.

DELMORE *(Mounting dread and panic)*: Oh, no . . .

HARRY *(Also laughing, caught up in the moment)*: Oh yes? Well, I always knew you were a girl with good judgment.

*(Rose and Harry laugh, Rose through her tears.)*

So, it's a deal, then?

ROSE: Oh, yes, Harry, it's a deal.

*(Harry picks up his glass of tea, Rose hers. They prepare for a toast.)*

ROSE *(Refers to glass)*: Oooh, it's hot . . .

HARRY: To us! . . .

ROSE: . . . And our exceptional future!

*(They're about ready to drink when Delmore exclaims:)*

DELMORE: DON'T!!

*(Rose and Harry stop. They look at him. The music also stops.)*

Don't do it!!

ROSE: Harry, what is he carrying on?

DELMORE *(Distraught)*: It's not too late to change your minds,
   both of you. There's still time . . .

HARRY: What are you getting so excited about?

DELMORE *(A beat)*: Your desserts . . . you can still change your
   orders! You can still have the chocolate layer cake! It's
   not too late!

HARRY *(To Rose)*: Don't pay any attention to him.

DELMORE: Please . . . there's still time . . .

ROSE: What's wrong with him?

HARRY: Crazy waiter.

DELMORE: Please . . .

HARRY: Ignore him.

   *(Harry raises his glass. Rose with an eye still on Delmore,
   lifts hers.)*

To us.

ROSE: To us.

   *(They touch glasses.)*

DELMORE *(Covers his eyes with his hands)*: Oh, no . . .

   *(Tableau: Rose and Harry in the middle of their toast. Rose
   is looking at Delmore, whose face is in his hands.
      Lights begin to fade except for the spots on their faces.
      Fade out. The sound of the ocean is heard in the darkness.)*


SCENE SIX

*A photographer's booth on the boardwalk.*
   *Rose and Harry are posed before a camera on a tripod. Delmore,
as the photographer, is hidden beneath the black drape of the camera.*
   *Delmore steps out from under the drape and assesses the pose. He
goes to Harry and arranges his hand on Rose's shoulder. Rose giggles.*

*Delmore carefully looks over the pose then thinks of an addition. He scurries to a corner and gets a bouquet of artificial flowers. Harry rolls his eyes exasperatedly. Delmore arranges the flowers in Rose's arms. Rose giggles.*

*Delmore hurries back under the drape. His hand protrudes clutching the rubber ball. It appears that he's about to take the picture when he decides not to and comes out from under the drape again.*

*Harry sighs impatiently; Rose giggles in an attempt to pacify him.*

*Delmore, meanwhile, is scrutinizing their pose: something about it isn't right. He thinks of something to correct it and scurries to another corner. He returns with a chair and seats Rose in it.*

*Delmore continually adjusts Rose's position on the chair. His perfectionism annoys Harry; Harry taps his foot in impatience.*

*Delmore finishes arranging Rose and then takes Harry's arm to place it properly. Harry violently yanks his arm from Delmore's hold and glares at him.*

*Delmore returns to the camera and goes beneath the drape. In a beat, he timidly pokes his head out to offer a new adjustment.*

HARRY *(Cutting Delmore off)*: Take the picture, dammit!

> *(Delmore squeezes the ball. A burst of light; the picture is taken.*
> *Tableau: Harry is frozen in an angry grimace, Rose's smile is uncomfortable and overcompensating.*
> *Silence.*
> *Blackout. The sound of the ocean is heard in the darkness.)*


### SCENE SEVEN

*A gypsy fortune teller's booth on the boardwalk.*

*Delmore, as the gypsy, is seated by a table on which is a crystal ball.*

*Rose and Harry enter, strolling on the boardwalk.*

ROSE: Oooh, Harry, let's get our fortune told!

HARRY: You don't really want to, do you?

ROSE: Yes. It would be fun. Come. We'll see what the future holds.

HARRY: Why would you want to do that?

ROSE: Aren't you even a little bit curious?

HARRY: No.

ROSE: Come on, Harry . . . Please . . .

HARRY: This is nonsense, Rose.

ROSE: It's only twenty-five cents.

HARRY: Twenty-five cents too much.

DELMORE: Fortune?

HARRY: Let's go.

ROSE *(Petulantly)*: No.

HARRY: All they do is make up lies and deceive people.

ROSE: I'm going in. Are you coming with me?

*(Pause. Harry begrudgingly follows her to the booth.)*

DELMORE: Twenty-five cents.

*(Rose looks to Harry; he fishes in his pocket for a quarter and hands it to Delmore. Delmore looks the coin over suspiciously, then pockets it.)*

*(To Rose)* Sit.

*(Rose sits expectantly. Delmore dramatically unveils the crystal ball; Harry rolls his eyes. Delmore moves his hands over the crystal ball, peers into it.)*

Hmm . . .

ROSE: Gypsy, what do you see?

DELMORE: It doesn't look good . . .

HARRY: What nonsense . . .

*(Rose shushes Harry.)*

DELMORE: Perhaps you don't want me to tell you what I see.

HARRY: You're right.

ROSE: No, tell me.

DELMORE: I see a future filled with remorse, hatred, scandal . . .

ROSE: What?

DELMORE: . . . lingering bitterness, deceit . . .

ROSE (Skeptical but good humored): That can't be . . .

HARRY: Utter nonsense . . .

DELMORE: I see a loss of fortune . . .

HARRY: Poppycock . . .

DELMORE: . . . destitution, infidelity, early death . . .

HARRY: Rose, it's a racket, come, let's go . . .

ROSE: Gypsy, do you have another crystal ball? You're giving someone else's fortune, not ours . . .

HARRY: These are nothing but children's toys! Crystal balls! Come, Rose . . .

ROSE: Gypsy, look into the ball again. Will we have children?

HARRY: Rose, I can't listen to this . . .

DELMORE: Yes, you will have children.

ROSE: Harry, listen . . .

DELMORE: A son . . .

ROSE: Harry, a son!

DELMORE: A son whose character will be monstrous.

ROSE: No, that can't be . . .

HARRY: Rose, I can't stand this anymore . . .

(Harry tugs Rose's arm and tries to pull her to her feet, she resists.)

DELMORE (To Harry): What's the matter? Can't you bear the truth?

HARRY: Truth?! This isn't truth, this is a terrible joke! You shouldn't be allowed to do this, you should be run off the boardwalk! Rose . . .

ROSE: I want the gypsy to look into another ball . . .

HARRY: Well, very well then, Rose, you do whatever you want . . .

*(Harry angrily strides out of the booth and off the stage.)*

ROSE *(Choking back tears; a shriek)*: Harry!! Harry, wait!!

*(Rose starts to run after Harry, but Delmore takes hold of her arm. Rose tries to break the hold but cannot. She looks at Delmore in confusion.)*

DELMORE: Don't.

*(Pause. Rose considers Delmore's request.)*

ROSE: Let go of my arm!
DELMORE: Don't go after him.
ROSE: I have to! What will I do if I don't go after him? Huh? Let go of me, I have to catch up with him!!

*(Pause. Delmore considers Rose's remark, then lets her go.)*

Harry, wait!! I'm coming!

*(Rose runs off, taking a final glimpse of Delmore before she exits.*
    *Delmore is alone. As the lights begin to fade, he takes off his costume, revealing the pajamas he wore in the first scene. He stands with his back to the audience.*
    *Fade out. The sound of a movie projector is heard in the darkness.)*

### SCENE EIGHT

*As in Scene One, the stage is empty except for a movie theatre seat in which Delmore sits facing the audience. There's an overturned box of popcorn at his feet. Tears stream down his cheeks.*

*A light flickers on the audience from behind Delmore.*

*We hear a crescendo of romantic music, signifying the end of the "movie."*

*In a beat, lights come full up. The Usher (played by the elder Rose, dressed as she was in Scene One) enters with a broom and dust pan and begins sweeping up the aisles of the theatre.*

USHER: A real tearjerker, huh? Don't you love the way she runs back to him at the end? I love happy endings.

DELMORE: You think that was a happy ending?

USHER: Sure, they both got what they wanted, didn't they.

DELMORE: Yes . . .

USHER: I mean, *he* wanted *her* and you could tell by the way she looked at him she was crazy about the guy. You've got to admit, the guy had a certain charm.

DELMORE: It had to be that way.

USHER: Yeah.

DELMORE: It *had* to be that way. It was fate.

USHER: Fate? Yeah, fate. Hand me that box of popcorn. *(He does)* Now, you better clear out of here . . .

DELMORE: Can't I stay for a little while longer?

USHER: No. I've got to close the place up.

DELMORE: Do you mind if I stay a little longer?

USHER: Yes, I mind.

DELMORE: It's very comfortable here.

USHER: I'm glad you like it but you can't stay.

DELMORE: Please, just a little longer.

USHER: Young man, you're being a nuisance.

DELMORE: I'll help you sweep up.

USHER: Look, it's time, do I have to throw you out myself?

DELMORE: I want to stay.

USHER: Well, you *can't* stay! You can't do whatever you want in this world, young man . . .

*(She pulls him out of the seat and begins to push him out.)*

Now, go, get out of here . . . Go!

*(She pokes him with the broom; Delmore exits. She looks off at him and shakes her head.*
*Fade out. Amplified sound of phonograph needle skipping on a record, as in the Prologue.)*


### EPILOGUE

*December 1934. The kitchen of the Schwartz apartment, the morning following the Prologue.*

*The skipping phonograph needle fades into the sound of a barely audible radio.*

*Rose sets two glasses with tea bags on the kitchen table. She carefully arranges the morning newspaper at one of the place settings. She warms her hands over a tea kettle on the stove then sits and looks out the window.*

*In a beat, Delmore enters; he's still wearing his pajamas. Rose senses his presence, turns to look at him, smiles, returns to the window.*

*Silence.*

ROSE: It snowed.

DELMORE: A lot?

ROSE: Enough. *(Pause)* I thought I'd let you sleep on account it's your birthday.

DELMORE: Thanks. *(Pause)* Good morning.

ROSE: Good morning. How does it feel to be twenty-one?

DELMORE: Cold.

ROSE: Put on some clothes you won't be cold. I put up some
water for tea.
DELMORE: Good.

*(Pause.)*

ROSE: The morning paper's here.
DELMORE: I see.
ROSE: I went out and got the paper.
DELMORE: In the snow?
ROSE: In the snow. So what. It's your birthday, I figured you'd
like to read the paper when you got up.
DELMORE: Thank you.
ROSE: Happy birthday.
DELMORE: Thanks.
ROSE: Twenty-one.
DELMORE: Yes. *(Pause)*
ROSE: So, are you glad to have the paper?
DELMORE: Very, yes.
ROSE: Good.

*(Pause.)*

DELMORE: Ma, I had a dream.
ROSE: A good dream? A bad dream?
DELMORE: I think I cried in my sleep.
ROSE: What did you dream that made you cry?

*(Pause. Delmore considers describing the dream to her but
decides not to.)*

DELMORE: I can't remember.
ROSE: If you can't remember, chances are it wasn't important.

*(A beat.)*

DELMORE: Ma, would you do something for me?
ROSE *(Unsure)*: Do something? What?

*(Delmore exits the kitchen.)*

*(Calls after him)* Where you going?! I put up water!

*(In a beat, Delmore returns carrying Rose's sewing basket; he extends it to her. At first she doesn't know why he's handing it to her, then recalls the discussion of her ripped sweater. Rose thinks it over, then takes the basket from him.*

*Delmore sits at the table. Rose takes off her sweater and joins him there. Soon Delmore becomes involved in reading the newspaper while Rose threads a needle and begins to mend her sweater.*

*The tea kettle whistles.*

*Fade out.)*

# MONOLOGUES

Many of the monologues and short pieces contained in this volume were written and developed while the author was a member of The New York Writers Bloc (1977–88), a group to which he is forever indebted.

*Louie*, *Anthony*, *Joey* and *Lola* were first presented as part of *Tuna on Rye and Other Short Pieces* in New York's Ensemble Studio Theater's 1983 Octoberfest. The plays were directed by Willie Reale and performed by Larry Block (Louie), Millard Corbett (Anthony), Keith Gordon (Joey) and Marcia Haufrecht (Lola).

# LOUIE

*An older, hearing-impaired man.*

LOUIE: I know how long ago it happened 'cause of that picture?
*From Here to Eternity?* When Pearl Harbor. Round there.
Pearl Harbor, there in Hawaii. *(Pause)* I was gonna
enlist. In the navy? Came out 4-F. They called me back a
year later anyways, guess to make sure I was still 4-F.
*(Pause)* I think it happened 'cause once on 34th Street?,
they were digging up the street. And I was crossing, waiting for the light. And I was standing right next to one of
those guys with the big noisy— *(Uses his hands to show a
jackhammer)* Y'know what I mean? Prolly not, though,
right? Nah. Prolly not. *(Pause)* Threw me outta school
'cause of it. Least if I'd've been nineteen, least I'd've had
a diploma from high school, least I'd've got a real job,
maybe. They dint wanna give what you call special attention. Nowadays it's different. I wanna go back to school.
I see in the paper they got this city college gives special
attention for deaf people. You think they would take me?
Huh? I got partial hearing. I can still hear a little with a
hearing aid. Like I could hear the lady next door sometimes. She yells, I hear her. *(Pause)* Like you, you speak
clear so I can talk to you. Some people, they turn their
heads, they expect me to hear! I say, "'Scuse me," or
"Par'n me." They're so dumb. The lipreading teacher said
the best thing is to talk to people who hear normal. Even
five minutes at a time. It's very important, she says. She
got married. Then she left again to have kids. You can't
talk to everybody, though, 'cause not everybody speaks
clear. *Five* minutes, even. *(Holds his outstretched palms up;*

*pause)* You can go a little nuts with so much no sound. Sometimes I turn it to Channel 13. Opera I can hear. Beverly Sills? Her I can hear. I can hear some of her sounds. Sometimes I can follow what's on the TV but I keep the voice part down. All that noise! I have to put the voice part all the way up to hear just a little bit so it's not worth all the noise. And the lady next door, she yells. *(Pause)* Take Crosby. I can't hear. Bing Crosby, he sings too low for me. Perry Como? Him, too. I can hear him singing, but I can't *hear* him. *(Pause)* Does that make sense? Sometimes I catch maybe it'll be a couple words. Y'know what that's like? Like tasting ice cream, you wanna hear more. *(Pause)* I wanna learn to take pictures. Photographer. *(Pause)* You think they'd give a driver's license to a deaf person? Prolly not. What if I put on big rearview mirrors? On both sides. Twice the size of regular ones. *(Pause)* The blind got it better. Yeah, they're better off. Least they can talk. Least they can put on a record.

# ANTHONY

*A twelve-year-old boy.*

ANTHONY: They called the cops. You should have been there.
Flashing lights and everything. And the honking, and all
the bright headlights, and the kids and everybody in the
street: "Jump! Jump!" Everybody was out of their house.
There was a big crowd. My father, he let me get up on his
shoulders so I saw everything great. I was the highest kid
there and I could see everything. I saw the hair of everybody in the crowd. And my little brother, Edward, he
cried because he wanted to see, too, but my father wouldn't
let him, he only let me. Because I'm older, and also
because when he saw what was really going on, he said to
my mother, "Irene, take Eddie upstairs, go on." Harlene's
mother was on the roof and she was screaming. She took
her shirt off so all you saw was her white skin and black
bra. She was screaming and she was crying but she was
too far up to hear and everybody was talking so loud until
she screamed, "Tommy!" Everybody got quiet. "Tommy!
Tommy!!" She was screaming. Tommy's the super.

Then Tommy got up there on the roof and you could
see him by his T-shirt sometimes because it looked white.
He was talking but you couldn't hear him. She yelled and
called him bad names. He said something else, also, you
couldn't hear what. She like walked to the edge of the
roof, you could see her standing there. She yelled, "I'm
gonna jump, don't go near me!" Everybody got real quiet
listening. Then, her shirt fell off the roof. Everybody
went: "Oh," all at the same time and some of the older
kids climbed the fence and took it out of the tree like they

55

were at a ball game. Harlene's mother looked down at us and everybody looked up and it got quiet again and Billy laughed.

And then you saw it: a cop came out of the dark on the roof and grabbed Harlene's mother and pulled her back into the dark and you couldn't see her anymore. Some of the older kids went: "Boo!" and some of the grown-ups got angry and some of them clapped. Everybody started to go home. My father bent down to get me off his shoulders. He told me I was breaking his back.

# JOEY

*A man in his early twenties.*

JOEY: They gave it, it was this big, I'm telling you. Juiciest
spare ribs you ever saw and special fried rice we ordered.
This big. No shit, big as this. They throw everything in
it, big chunks of *pork* they throw in, egg, whatayacallem,
*peas* . . . Vinnie, he wolfs down an egg roll like he's Linda
Lovelace or something. You should see him. Duck sauce
all over his chin. Fucking pig. There was lots and lots of
food. Kept on ordering and ordering like there's no
tomorrow. What the fuck did I care? I wasn't laying out
for it, shit, it was my fucking birthday. Bill came to like
fifty bucks or something, I don't know, sixty maybe. But,
oh man, this Wing's Palace, they got like the best fucking
egg foo yong you will ever eat in your entire life, I mean
if you like egg foo yong. And Douglas? He got like the
number six whatayacallem? combo jobs? Wing's Palace
special chow mein. They throw *lob*ster in it, *spare* ribs,
*pork* they got, uh, *shrimp*, *spare* ribs, you name it it's in
there. We was all like sharing food, me, Vinnie, William,
and this faggot Douglas was guarding his plate like it was
Fort Knox or something. We was all like eating off each
other's plate, you know tasting here and there?, except for
Douglas who, I'm telling you, is acting like a faggot.
Everybody else is like sharing, having a good time, swig-
ging the six-pack from under the table, making a mess
when you open the can and the beer sprays the old couple at the next booth, and the Chink he's getting like real
upset, his fucking floor is sticky from beer, I mean it's
really worth it to have a heart attack over spilled beer,

right? This is a school night, I might add. And me? Fuck them, I figured why not, I order the most expensive thing on the menu: Wing's Palace Lobster Deluxe. I die from lobster. I figured what the shit, I'm the birthday boy, I deserve it. Shit, I'm like a father to these boys. I mean, it is *real* expensivo but so what? Douglas, naturally, right? Douglas puts up a stink: "Who the fuck you think you are," blah blah blah. I mean, this is an asshole. This is a useless piece of dick. Douglas, with a memory like a retarded elephant, is telling me *who-the-fuck-are-you.* I mean—and this is not a long time ago—Douglas, and I might add, this Douglas is no Robert Redford— Douglas, he's trying so fucking hard it was pathetic to make out with this nothing-tease he meets, I don't know, some girl he meets somewheres. When his cousin got married he picked her up at the wedding, something like that. This is out in *Rock*ville he goes, he couldn't find a girl in Sheepshead Bay or something more local, no, he has to go allaway out to fucking Rockville *Cen*tre just to like get his rocks off on this nothing chick, Roberta her name was. You think *I* got bad skin? Man, you should see *her.* Zits like *dimes* man, *this* big, no shit, all over her head. So what happens he goes allaway out to Rockville fucking Centre? Guess. You got it. She don't want to have nothing to do with him if you know what I mean. Is this a nothing tease or what? I advised him on this in the very very beginning. I told him, "Douglas, lay off this Roberta. I know girls like this from personal experience," I told him, "they were put on this earth to turn balls blue, forget her." He don't listen to his friend Joey, naturally, and this Roberta like slaps his hands and says: "Nothing doing, dildo," so Douglas, he's like in this parking lot in this *mall* out in *Rock*ville with blue marbles in his pants, a tease in the front seat won't have nothing to do with him, and his fucking car like *dies* on him. Cardiac arrest, man. Poof! The thing won't fart to save his life. So what does he do? He calls me up fucking collect from this pay phone in this shopping mall in Rockville Centre, Long Island. And me! I accept the charge like an asshole. And he don't *ask*: "Can you do me a favor and so and so," no, the prick *tells* me: "Joey you gotta come get me." I *gotta*. Do you believe this? It's fucking one A.M. My old lady got real pissed and I don't blame her, I mean who likes getting a call from an asshole at one o'clock in the morning? And William was over the house. We was getting stoned on the porch whenever there was a commercial. *Saturday Night Live* is really beginning to suck. So, anyway, like a total asshole, I don't say: "Douglas, fuck off," no, so me and William, who is even more wrecked than me, me and William we get into my car—do not ask me why I do this please—and we take this ride out to this fucking stupid absolute dildo in a dead car in a parking lot in Rockville fucking Centre, Long Island. And I'm driving there and driving there and I am seeing triple and I'm screaming at William: "What the sign say? Tell me what the sign say," and he keeps saying: "Slow down, Joe, I can't read them." I'm telling you, this is what I have to put up with. Finally, I mean after all this, we find the stupid fucking shopping mall and there's Douglas, sleeping on the steering wheel like a drunk driver or something. Girl skipped out on him, poor prick. So what do I do? Jump his car, straighten him out, give him a little pep talk (you know, like don't take it so hard, she was a nothing tease from the word go). I follow right behind him on the highway, make sure he don't decide to jump lanes and kill himself or anything, take him home to his mother and practically tuck him in. Did this fucking asshole ever once say to me: "Thanks a lot, Joey," or "Joe, what a friend." Huh? *(Pause)* So what the fuck if I order lobster?

# LOLA

*A Polish refugee. Lightly, animatedly.*

LOLA: I met my husband Liberation Day. I lost my *sister* Liberation Day. I don't know how she dies, but she does. On Liberation Day. A lot of people lost people Liberation Day. The mourning period was very short in those days—if you planned on surviving. No time for shiva. If there was time for shiva, oh God, we all would've died. There was so much of it: death. All over the place. And, my sister, who I'll tell you I happened to love very much, *very* much. I never saw her again. What could I do? By that time, Papa, Mama, my brother Izzy who was never too smart, they were all dead. Not *me*, and there was nothing I could do about it; right? What could I have done, this little pip-squeak? That's what I looked like when my husband met me. I was a real *meiskeit*. You know what that means in Jewish? Uh . . . uh . . . what you kids, my daughter, calls a real loser: "Oh, Ma, is that Sharon a real loser." *(A beat)* I looked a real *meiskeit* because I almost lost my life, that's why. Auschwitz wasn't Grossinger's, honey. Three meals a day? Forget it! Shuffleboard? Go on! You've read about it, I'm sure. Well, it was worse than that, believe me, and I got there like at the tail end. They stopped giving numbers by the time I got there. They must've run out of numbers. Like at the bakery. You notice I don't have numbers on my arm? Well, that's the reason: they ran out of 'em. *(A beat)* So, I was a *meiskeit*. I wasn't the beauty I am today. I had typhoid. My teeth were falling out. I was very skinny, as you could imagine. Knock-kneed. So, between the teeth missing

65

and my knees knocking, I was not your typical bathing-suit beauty. But my husband, I don't know, somehow he saw something. You see, he comes up to me Liberation Day. Somebody points me out to him: "Go, look, that girl there, she's from Lodz." That's where I lived before the camps. Turns out my husband, he, too, lived in the Lodz ghetto. I didn't know him. But, wait, I'll tell you—he comes up to me, a good-looking guy, not too tall, I look him up and down: Hmm, I think to myself, Not bad. He says to me: "Excuse me, I hear you're from the Lodz ghetto." I nodded. I didn't want to keep my mouth open too much, this good-looking guy might see all my teeth that fell out, so I nodded uh-huh. "Tell me," he said, "I'm looking for someone. From Lodz. Can you tell me if you happen to know if she's alive? Her name is Lola. She is a beautiful girl with a magical smile and a sense of humor you could *plotz*. Tell me," he said, "do you know if she survived?" I asked him what street does this Lola live on in the ghetto. He told me. It was my street. And what address? He told me. It was my address. And what was the last name of her family? *(A beat)* "That's me!" I screamed, all of the spaces in my magical smile showing. "That's me! I am Lola!" And he carried me away, and, like the whole thing was a dream . . . I woke up: a housewife in Flatbush making gefilte fish for her family. A boy and a girl. Today, that boy has a daughter named for my sister, and the girl, the girl is a clinical psychologist.

# MANNY

*Manny* was commissioned and first presented by The Passage Theatre Company in Trenton, New Jersey, on June 20, 1986. It was directed by Brian Delate and performed by Thomas G. Waites.

*A twenty-five-year-old man.*

MANNY: You just come from the bathroom? You look like a guy
just come from the bathroom. You saw what went *on* in
there? Oh, these kids, these black kids, took a briefcase.
About this big. Brown. Leather, *you* know.

Guy in a business suit, a *lawyer*, sonofabitch is a lawyer
I bet. *Looked* like a lawyer. I've seen *lawyers* looked like
that. He was drunk. He was drinking. Comes off the
train, he can't hold it. I'm standing up taking a leak.
Sonofabitch runs in, can't hold it. Drops his briefcase.
*Out*side the john, *you* know, with the door? Leaves his
thing *out*side and shuts the door! What a jackass thing to
do! I see him doing this and I think: this guy is asking for
it. A *lawyer*. These guys you expect would know better,
but no. So, he's in there farting and belching, trying to
get his drunk piss flowing, and these two black kids come
in and I think: uh-oh, trouble.

One-two-three, that briefcase is *gone*. Those little pricks
are off and running. I knew it. The second they came in.
I can tell these things. The sonofabitch comes out wetting
himself, fixing his belt, his face pink like a heart attack,
and he's screaming: "Hey! I got my money in there!"

What kind of fucking asshole *attorney* does something as
stupid as putting his money in a thing and leaving it *out*-
side the john? No wonder he gets ripped off. What a way
to go through life.

This friend of mine? Had this gun. Not me, it was his. I don't have no gun. The service, yeah. The army, yes. I'm talking *civilian* y'understand. Civilian. I don't use guns. I don't *shoot* guns. Oh, yeah, once. Went hunting. Upstate New York. Hunting, like for deers. Wasn't the season, though. Just shot at things. *You* know, like for practice. Target practice. Beer cans and shit.

Aside from that, besides that, I never had a gun on my *person* before. Except for this time with this friend. I got busted. He carries a gun, this friend. Like for protection. I'm not gonna tell you his name 'cause you may know him and I want to respect his privacy.

It's a very small world. You never know. I'm very careful about these things. I don't say names in restaurants 'cause you never know who's sitting behind you. (This is how I go through life.) You may know him and he may not want you knowing this, so don't ask me his name 'cause I ain't telling. His name is irrevelent. [*Sic*] I'll tell you *my* name. 'Cause I don't care. I'm *talk*ing to you. Got your face memorized. I'll remember you next time I see you. I'm good at that. But *him?*, my friend? Forget it. I ain't telling. Me? I'm Manny. Nice to meet you, too.

So, this is 'round Christmas I'm talking about. My friend, he shows me this gun. Like we were hanging out his place watching wrestling or something? He shows me this gun, right? And I go, "Hey, man, you got a gun? Let's go stick somebody up." I'm kidding, right? And he goes, "You want?" And, like, I'm smiling but I'm not really? You know what I mean? Like I'm thinking: is he kidding or what? And he goes, "Let's go out." And I go, "It's cold out, man, it's Christmas." He goes, "Exactly." And I think to myself: shit, this is like two days before

Christmas . . . I could use some extra bucks. *Pre*sents and stuff. Everybody could use a little extra 'round the holidays. *You* know how it is. My girlfriend just so happened to be pregnant at the time, so, *you* know, I wanted to like give her something to cheer her up. *Christmas* and everything. I mean, there was a certain logic to it. We weren't gonna *hurt* nobody. Just scare. I don't hurt nobody 'less I have to. I don't go out of my way in other words.

So we went out. Not too cold, but cold. I was wearing a, you know, reddish coat, and my friend's gun, it was in my pocket. I loaded it personally. Only two or three bullets in there, tops. Not six. Definitely not six. And we go down to Dwight Street. And we hang out in this lot? Near the pizza place? And we're waiting. And waiting. People go. Couples. Too complicated.

And we wait. And it's getting cold. And then I see this lady coming. Carrying packages. You know: shopping bags. Presents. And I say to Rudy, "Let's go." And we come out of the lot and I go, "Give me your presents and (*you* know) your pocketbook." And she starts giving us a hard time. Says her husband's watching from the window. "Bull*shit*." "He's watching," she goes. And Rudy goes. (Shit!) My *friend* goes, "Look, lady, we just want your presents and your money. Don't be stupid." And she goes, "I will not! Blah-blah-blah-blah-blah!" And she's yelling and I'm thinking: shit. And he goes, "Lady, shut up or we're gonna shoot you." And she yells. And I think: what if a police car comes? I mean, they *do*. A police car *is* gonna come by sooner or later. I *am* a logical person. So I go to my friend, I go, "Let's quit this shit." And I tell the lady, "Listen, I won't kill you this time. But just don't call the cops, okay?" And she goes, "Yes, yes, of course." And we go. And I say to her, "Merry Christmas, lady."

Cops picked us up two blocks later. Bitch went ahead and told them. She tells! I spared her life and she tells! I wished her a Happy New Year and everything! Shit.

Got off easy. Dumped the gun. But still . . .What a way to go through life. Can't trust nobody. Got to look out every second.

I been a victim. I know about these things. I was mugged myself. I was opening up my car. Two guys come up to me like out of nowheres. White guys. They got a knife. You see this scar? Cut my whole face open. Like you could peel my whole skin off. Cut me deep. The blood was amazing. I chased *after* the scumbag. Other guy got away. I went after the scumbag who cut me.

*Never run away from them.*
*Make them run away from you.*

I caught up with this guy. I couldn't see 'cause of the blood, but I grabbed him and knocked him down on the ground. And I whipped out this hammer, see. I had this hammer on me. I whipped out this hammer and bam! bam! Hit him in the head. Bam! Bam! More and more and more. Couldn't stop. Like it was uncontrollable. I had no control over it. Bam! Bam! Bam! Till his head, you could stuff tomatoes in it.

Self-defense. I got off. Fucking lawyer almost did me in, the sonofabitch. Lawyers.

What a way to go through life.

# I DON'T KNOW
# WHAT I'M DOING

*For Didi Conn*

*A woman in her thirties.*

NANCY: Excuse me, I don't know what I'm doing. I bought a one-way ticket for Madison. I've never been to Wisconsin. I know one person in the whole state. Is it cold this time of year? I didn't think. I got on the plane with an overnight bag. Just my toothbrush and a change of undies, practically. I don't know what I'm doing; I can't believe I'm doing this. *(A beat)* I'm going to see an old friend. For a visit. But it's sort of a surprise. I mean it *is* a surprise because he doesn't know I'm coming. I hope he's there; I've got an address. *(Takes out an envelope with letter)* True, the letter's from 1979, but I'm hoping he didn't move around much. How big can Madison *be?* *(A beat)* This was the letter I got from him, congratulating me on my wedding. He said that by the time his mother forwarded the invitation to him it was too late for him to come but that that was alright 'cause he didn't think he would've come anyway. *(Reads from letter)* "If you picked Steve out of all the guys in the world, he must be one terrific guy." Ha. "Have a good life, Nancy. Be fruitful, etcetera. Remember me always and I'll do the same for you. Billy. P.S. Save me a piece of wedding cake." *(Puts letter back in envelope)*

Billy and I used to play married. In high school, we'd cut out and go to his house after his mother went to work and take off our clothes and get under the covers of his parents' double bed and roll around each other. We never did it; he never tried; I took that as a sign of how much he loved me. But I'd lie on top of him, naked, and we'd

75

talk about everything, *every*thing—school, friends, Janis
Joplin, mothers and fathers—and whisper and laugh, and
feel our breaths get hot, and we'd lie like that for hours,
till we were tired and sweaty, and then we'd take a shower
together. We'd do that all the time it seemed, but maybe
it was just a couple of times. I would hang out in front of
school and wait for him, right before I'd have to go into
homeroom, wait for him with my heart pounding in my
ears, hoping he'd show up and take me back to his parents' bed and take off my clothes and talk to me. He
talked to me like nobody else. Like nobody else before or
since. The sound of his voice wrapped me up like a blanket. I could lay in his voice forever, soft and warm, his
breath on me.

*(A beat.)*

He had the littlest tush, Billy; his pants would hang in the
back where his tush should be. And his eyes were small
and brown but they always *looked* at you. Some people
even with big eyes don't, they don't really *look* at you.
I made him laugh. He told me I was beautiful.

*(A beat.)*

We slept on the beach one night before we graduated,
Brighton Beach. Under the boardwalk where the sand
was cold and didn't smell like sand. You could see the
moonlight through the slats on the sand. You could hear
somewhere out in the dark some kids going at it, and the
ocean, and sometimes people walking up above and the
wood creaking. And I lay on top of Billy, with our
clothes on, and whispered and laughed till we both fell
asleep, tired from all that wonderful talk. I woke up at
that strange hour when the sky isn't quite morning yet,
and you happen to be up when the streetlights click off?

We didn't plan to fall asleep, it just happened. When I got home it was around 5:30 and my father was sitting in his chair in his underwear smoking a cigarette and my mother was snoring on the sofa. My father was so mad at me he didn't even yell. He cried. He sobbed. "How could you do this?" he said, over and over. "Nancy, Nancy, Nancy. How could you do this?" And I said, "I don't know what I'm doing." I wanted to tell him we were talking, me and Billy, we were only talking, but instead I told him I didn't know what I was doing.

*(A beat.)*

My father made it very hard for me to see Billy again after that. We graduated and I went to Brooklyn College and he went upstate, to Binghamton. The next time I saw him was Thanksgiving of our freshman year when he came home. I was with my family and he was with his, and we were going into a Chinese restaurant on Ocean Avenue and they were just leaving. We were like Romeo and Juliet, our parents muttering hellos and looking at each other funny as we walked past like the enemy. I thought I would die, that my heart would stop pumping and I would collapse and die. That night I called him and snuck out of the house and met him at the boardwalk. I didn't care what would happen, I had to see him. He was stoned when he got there, and his little eyes were puffy and bloodshot, and his beautiful voice was hoarse from all that smoke. He didn't sound like Billy anymore. We went under the boardwalk. I had so much to tell him, so much to talk to him about. It was November and freezing, not like it was in May, and he got on top of *me* this time. This time he didn't want to talk.

*(Pause.)*

I can't blame him. It was my fault he was the way he was. If I'd stood up to my father and told him nothing happened that night, if I'd only told him all we did was talk, I would've still been allowed to see Billy and he wouldn't've gotten stoned, and the thing that happened that night wouldn't've happened. I ran home hysterical. My father heard my crying and knocked on my door and asked, very nicely really, if I was okay; he asked like he knew what happened, but I wanted to tell him all about it anyway but I didn't and he went back to bed.

*(Pause.)*

This tall, skinny, sort of cute boy in my Intro to Drama class, who had been asking me out every couple of weeks and I kept putting him off and putting him off, well, he asked me again the Monday after Thanksgiving if I would go out with him and I said yes. He had big green eyes and his name was Steve and four years later I married him.

*(Pause; she takes a wedge of something wrapped in tinfoil out of her bag.)*

Nine-year-old wedding cake. I kept it in my freezer, moved five times with it packed in dry ice. It can't taste like much, but that's not the point. Billy asked me to save him a piece. *(Pause; her eyes suddenly fill with tears, she smiles brightly and blushes)* I still love him. *(She shrugs)*

# SHORT PLAYS

# FATHER AND SON

*Father (fifties) and Son (twenties) seated at a table in an apartment, looking over a checkbook and check ledger.*

FATHER: And what do I put here?

SON: The amount.

FATHER: I get it.

SON: You put in the amount, then you subtract it from the balance.

FATHER: Which is the balance?

SON: The balance. The total you start out with.

FATHER: I get it. So the amount goes here.

SON: Right.

FATHER: And then I subtract the amount from the balance.

SON: Right.

FATHER: So let's say I'm paying Con Ed. Here I write "Con Ed" and where it says amount, I put in how much the check is for.

SON: Right.

FATHER: And then I subtract the amount from the balance. How'm I doing?

SON: Great.

FATHER: This isn't so hard. All those years I thought your mother was doing something so hard and mysterious. This isn't bad at all. I'm doing okay, right?

SON: You're doing great.

FATHER: I'm not such a bad student, am I?

SON: No, it's just that I'm such a good teacher.

FATHER *(Laughs)*: So anyway, what do I do after I subtract?

SON: Nothing.

FATHER: So what's this number here?

SON: Your new balance.

FATHER: Oh. And then what do I do? I go on to the next check?

SON: Right. And you just do the same thing for each check.

FATHER: I get it. So let's say I write a check out to the phone company.

SON: It's the same procedure.

FATHER: I write in the amount, subtract it, and then I wind up with . . . I forgot what you called it.

SON: The new balance.

FATHER: Right. And that's all there is to it. That's how you balance a checkbook. Gee.

SON: Well, I gotta go.

FATHER: What time is it?

SON: It's almost seven.

FATHER: Gee, I had no idea.

SON: I don't want to get home too late. The trains are crazy.

FATHER: No, of course not. It'll probably be dark by the time you get home.

SON: Yeah, I know.

FATHER: Well, let me just ask you something.

SON: What?

FATHER: What if I want to write *you* a check?

SON: What do you mean?

FATHER: Do I have to write your whole name in here? *(Meaning the ledger)*

SON: No.

FATHER: I don't?

SON: No. Nobody's gonna be looking at the book but you.

FATHER: So if I wrote you a check, all I really have to write in here is "Mickey," right? I don't have to write Michael Weiss or anything.

SON: No.

FATHER: I see. I can just write "Mickey" and that'll do.

SON: Dad, I really should go.

FATHER: Of course.

SON *(Kisses him)*: Take it easy.

FATHER: Naturally. How'm I doing?

SON: You're doing great.

FATHER: Hey, how's your girlfriend?

SON: Fine.

FATHER: She gets more beautiful every time I see her.

SON: Yeah . . . well, I'll speak to you soon.

FATHER: You gonna get the train right here?

SON: Yup.

FATHER: And that'll take you straight to your house?

SON: Uh, yeah, then I walk two blocks.

FATHER: Uh-huh. Okay.

SON: So, you can call me, too, you know.

FATHER: I will . . .

SON *(Kisses him)*: So take it easy.

FATHER: Hey, Mick?

SON: What?

FATHER: Come on, I'll take you home. *(Stands)*

SON: No.

FATHER: I don't want you on the trains. You could get killed.

SON: I ride the trains all the time, don't worry about it.

FATHER: Let me just get my stuff, go to the john . . .

SON: Forget about it. *60 Minutes* is almost on.

FATHER: So what, I can live without Mike Wallace.

SON: But you love *60 Minutes*.

FATHER: Ah, it's stupid lately. Let me pee.

SON: No, Dad, I'm going.

FATHER: What're you gonna do, such a long train ride.

SON: I've got the puzzle, I'll be fine.

FATHER: The crossword? Your mother was crazy about crosswords. She'd know all the answers one-two-three. *(Pause)*

SON: Look, this is really silly, Dad, what are you gonna start shlepping to the city for?, you've got a great spot.

FATHER *(A beat)*: Are you sure?

SON: Yes.

85

FATHER: Go already, then. I'd have to stop for gas anyway, so go.

SON: Yeah.

FATHER: You better get going.

SON: So long. *(Kisses him, they hug)*

FATHER: Your mother would have loved your haircut.

# DEATH IN
# THE FAMILY

*A telephone conversation.*
  *Mickey is in his twenties; Irving is in his fifties.*

MICKEY: Hello?
IRVING: Mickey, this is your Unc.
MICKEY: Hello.
IRVING: How are ya?
MICKEY: How are *you*?
IRVING: Listen: there was a death in the family.
MICKEY: Who?
IRVING: Sidney Grund.
MICKEY: Who's Sidney Grund?
IRVING: I don't know, a cousin of mine and your father's.
MICKEY: You're sure?
IRVING: Yeah, I think so. Listen: I'm calling you to tell your
    father, so, you tell him a cousin of his died. The funeral's
    tomorrow, 12:30, Parkside Chapel. You writing this
    down?
MICKEY: No.
IRVING: Tomorrow, 12:30, Parkside. Write it down.
MICKEY: Are you going?
IRVING: Nah. I don't even know who the guy is. To tell you the
    honest truth, I don't remember the guy. Jack says he's
    our cousin, he's our cousin. You have an uncle lives three
    blocks from you. Talk about families. Jack called me and
    told me to get in touch with Bob so that's why I called
    you. Your father gets annoyed—I know this—when
    nobody tells him when somebody dies. So, tell him:
    Sidney Grund is being buried tomorrow at Parkside,
    12:30. That's the place my wife was buried from. You

know, I always said I wanted to be buried standing up, and, you know?, I happen to read this article in the paper: there's a tribe somewheres, they bury their people standing up.

MICKEY: You planning on trying it?

IRVING: Nah. So, how's Bob?

MICKEY: Not so hot.

IRVING: How come?

MICKEY: You know how come.

IRVING: He should get himself a nice girl.

MICKEY: When he's ready.

IRVING: They don't make them like your mother. She was one in a million. He needs a nice girl to listen to him. I know. Me, I look at a girl, she looks at me. She says, Oooh, you're too fat, or too this. Sure I'm fat. Or, I'm too old. Nobody's interested in an old man.

MICKEY: How old are you, Irving?

IRVING: Fifty-eight.

MICKEY: That's very old.

IRVING: Sure it is. They think I'm too old. They don't bother with me, I don't bother with them. What can I tell you? So, you married yet?

MICKEY: No.

IRVING: Why not?

MICKEY: I'm too young for that sort of thing.

IRVING: You've got time.

MICKEY: I hope so.

IRVING: I was married twenty years. It wasn't the greatest. It had its ups and downs. You fight, you make up. It wasn't a bad way to spend twenty years. I don't regret nothing. The first four years, though . . . They were the greatest. So, do me a favor, tell your father what I told you. You write it down?

MICKEY: No.

IRVING: What I say?

MICKEY: 12:30, Parkside, tomorrow.

IRVING: You sure you didn't write it down? You got a good memory then. I had to write it down. I don't remember nothing. I'm not a bad guy, I got a bad memory. I'm not a bad guy. Believe me, if I really could've afforded it, I'd've had you over the house. Like the Italians, they're all close and live on top of each other, I would've had you over the house. You make a little more money than a brother, already they're calling you a *goniff*. So just tell your father. Okay? And tell him his big brother told him he doesn't have to go if he doesn't wanna. 'Bye. Just tell him what I told you. So long.

MICKEY: So long.

# NEW YEAR'S EVE
## AND
# KIBBUTZ

*New Year's Eve* and *Kibbutz* are two scenes from an abandoned play, *Heartbreaker*. It was commissioned by South Coast Repertory and developed at the Sundance Institute Playwrights' Conference in July 1989, where it featured Evan Handler as Jonathan, Daniel Jenkins as Bruce, Katherine Hiler as Paula and Kevin Kling as Yakov. After a workshop at SCR in November 1989, the play was shelved, but some of its scenes (not those included here) served as the basis for the play *Sight Unseen*.

*Lights up: The den of a middle-class house in Flatbush, Brooklyn. 1969. Wood-paneling, well-nourished plants. Judaic ornaments dress the walls, with framed family photos. An electric menorah is fully lit in the window; its orange light and the bluish cast of the television illuminate two figures on the sofa: Jonathan and Paula, both fifteen going on sixteen. She is a frizzy-haired Earth Mother, braless in her father's shirt. She has been crying. The TV is tuned to a Fred Astaire–Ginger Rogers movie. Jonathan and Paula sit side by side, her hand stroking his inner thigh, his fondling her breast. They seem to be moving in slow-motion while their eyes remain on the TV. Behind the sofa and to their left is an archway that leads to another part of the house; upstairs a party is going on. A bottle of wine is on the coffee table in front of them. Jonathan, already drunk, occasionally takes a swig to fortify his pursuit. This goes on for a while, until Bruce appears. He is the same age, slightly built; his hair is too short for him to pass as a hippie, although he wears jeans and wire-rimmed glasses. He stands in the doorway and secretly watches them in silence. After a long beat, he quietly sidles beside Paula and begins to fondle her thigh. Jonathan is unaware of his presence. Bruce, too, looks straight ahead at the TV, but gradually becomes engrossed in it.*

BRUCE *(Guessing)*: *Top Hat?*
JONATHAN *(Surprised)*: Bruce!—
BRUCE: Charles Walters. Nineteen thirty . . . eight.
JONATHAN: Mark Sandrich, '35—
BRUCE: Close.
JONATHAN: What do you want?

BRUCE: Everybody's wondering where you two went. I'm the posse. It's T-minus ten minutes to the new decade. Don't you want to come up and watch the ball drop?

*(Paula starts weeping again, takes the wine bottle from Jonathan and drinks.)*

What's with Paula?

JONATHAN: Leave us alone.

BRUCE: Paula?

JONATHAN: She's depressed.

BRUCE: Why're you depressed?

JONATHAN: She's *depressed*. I'm *comforting* her.

BRUCE: *Com*forting her?! You call this *comf*—?!

JONATHAN: Bruce . . . !

PAULA: I hate New Year's.

JONATHAN *(To Bruce)*: Would you leave us alone please?

BRUCE: But don't you want to watch the little ball?

JONATHAN: We want to watch this.

PAULA *(In utter seriousness)*: New Year's always does this to me. Worse than my birthday. It's something about seeing that new date on the newspaper the next morning. 1969 is gone forever. The sixties are gone forever. And there's nothing we can do to stop it. Nothing. We can't control it. It's bigger than us. It's like we're on a roller coaster and there's no stopping it. It's all going so fast all of a sudden, isn't it? We're getting old. *(She starts sobbing again)*

JONATHAN *(Gently amused)*: Paula, we're barely sixteen . . .

PAULA: Don't laugh at me!

JONATHAN: I'm not laughing!

PAULA: It's happening so fast all of a sudden! It is! It's accelerating! *(Bruce and Jonathan chortle)* Don't laugh! Didn't this year go faster than last year? Didn't '68 go by faster than '67?

JONATHAN: Are you asking me?

PAULA: It's spinning out of our hands! Spinning and spinning, faster all the time! Our youth is disappearing! That's right, laugh at me. Soon we'll be in college, then we'll be married, then we'll be divorced, then we'll be dead. I don't want to die . . .

*(She breaks down sobbing. Jonathan holds her and glares at Bruce to leave them alone. Pause. Bruce stays.)*

BRUCE: Are you still stoned from before? I think I am. Are you supposed to have like this amazing headache right here?

JONATHAN *(Confidentially to Bruce, regarding Paula)*: She must be having her p—

PAULA: I am not! God!

JONATHAN: You said yourself, you only get like this when you have your—

PAULA: Like what? Emotional? You mean otherwise I'm not emotional? I need a hormone imbalance to—

JONATHAN *(Over "imbalance to—")*: No, no . . . Shhh . . . Shut up. *(Suddenly looks queasy)*

PAULA: What.

JONATHAN: I don't feel so good.

PAULA: Put your head down.

JONATHAN *(Tries it)*: That's worse.

BRUCE: Are you gonna be sick?

JONATHAN *(Trying to concentrate his nausea away)*: Just leave me alone.

PAULA: Are you?

JONATHAN: Leave me *alone!*

BRUCE *(To Paula)*: He is.

JONATHAN: Bruce . . .

*(Pause.)*

BRUCE *(To Paula)*: You want to go up?

PAULA *(Shakes her head no; to Jonathan)*: How do you feel now?

JONATHAN: Shhh . . .

PAULA: If you're gonna be sick, do me a favor and puke on my parents' bed. Do it right on the George Washington bedspread.

*(Bruce changes the channel.)*

Put that back.

BRUCE: I just wanted to see—

PAULA: Put it back. If you want to watch the ball drop—

*(Bruce flips back to the movie.)*

Thank you. *(Pause. To Jonathan)* How ya doin'?

JONATHAN: Well, I wouldn't recommend kissing me right now . . .

*(Bruce and Paula laugh; Jonathan doesn't realize how funny that sounded, and he laughs, too. For a moment, they're all convulsed with laughter but a new wave of nausea hits Jonathan and he stumbles to his feet.)*

Uh-oh . . .

*(Jonathan wavers a moment, then hurries through the doorway. Paula starts to go after him.)*

PAULA: Jonathan? . . .

*(Bruce stops her by taking her hand. She looks at him for a beat.)*

BRUCE: Let him. *(A beat)* He wouldn't want you watching him, *you* know . . .

*(Pause. She joins him on the sofa. Silence, except for the TV, is broken by the sound of party revelers upstairs counting down from ten to the new year. Paula begins to cry again. Bruce watches her for a moment, not knowing what to do.)*

Paula?

PAULA: Nothing's the same anymore. My parents . . .

BRUCE: Shhh . . .

*(Pause. He kisses her wet cheek, her brow, her eyes, her nose. They look at each other for a long beat as the offstage revelers hoot and cheer in celebration. Paula suddenly kisses him, long and deep. As quickly as she kissed him, she resumes watching the movie. Bruce is perplexed but watches also. Still crying, her hand moves up his leg. He unbuttons her shirt and slips his hand inside as lights fade to black.)*

# KIBBUTZ

*Lights up: a sun-drenched orchard on a kibbutz in the Israeli desert. 1972. Bruce, seventeen, wearing a bandanna around his head, cut-offs and a soiled white T-shirt, sits on the ground among several baskets full of peaches. He has made a writing surface of his army surplus shoulder bag, on which he composes a blue air-mail letter. Nearby is a small knapsack belonging to Jonathan.*

*It is quiet. Birds pass overhead; Bruce looks up and tracks them, then writes about them in his letter.*

*Soon, Yakov, a twenty-two-year-old, brawny, brown-skinned Israeli, shiny with sweat, runs very quickly past Bruce and offstage.*

YAKOV *(Without stopping)*: Hey!! What are you *doing?*!! Up up up!

*(Yakov exits. Bruce watches him run in the distance, then returns to his letter. In a beat, Jonathan, also seventeen, wearing shorts and a Midwood High School T-shirt, enters. Flushed and perspired, he struggles with a bushel of freshly picked fruit and sets it down. Bruce hardly looks up from his writing.)*

JONATHAN: Who was *that?*
BRUCE *(Still not looking up)*: *You* know.
JONATHAN: Yakov? *(No response)* Bruce? Yakov?
BRUCE: I think. Yeah.

*(Pause. Thick with tension.)*

JONATHAN: These Israelis. Boy. They're perfect machines. Strong to the finish. Yeah. A nation of Popeyes. All that matzoh and Coca-Cola. They don't sweat, these guys. No, they *glisten*. Like Kirk Douglas in *Spartacus*. Even the women. Incredible muscle definition.

BRUCE *(Trying to concentrate on his letter)*: Jonathan . . .

JONATHAN: What. You're trying to write? Oooh, sorry.

*(Jonathan stretches out. Very long pause.)*

Who you writing to?

BRUCE: Paula.

JONATHAN *(Sarcastically)*: Really? Again? That was a dumb question. Boy is *she* gonna have some collection by the time we come home. All those air-letters . . . I run out of things to say on a *post*card. How could you be so full of things to say? *(Bruce looks annoyed again)* I mean, how come you have so much to say and I have to write really big to fill a postcard? It's funny, that's all. *(Pause)* What are you writing?

BRUCE: Jonathan . . .

JONATHAN: No, tell me: what are you *writing*? You don't have to *read* it to me or anything, I'm just curious. What types of things do you talk about?

BRUCE: What "types"?

JONATHAN: Yeah, you don't have to *read* it to me, I'm just curious.

BRUCE: I'm writing about our trip.

JONATHAN: Well, I figured as much.

BRUCE: Like a journal.

JONATHAN: Oh. Well. I write in my *journal* like a journal. So, in other words, instead of writing in a journal, you're making all these pithy observations to *Paula*. *("Pithy" angers Bruce)* I mean, not "pithy" . . . *You* know: smart, clever.

*(They look at one another for a long beat, then Bruce returns to his letter. Jonathan takes his sketchbook and a watercolor*

*box out of his knapsack and sets up to sketch a landscape.
Pause.)*

You know, we used to tell each *other* our stupid theories
of life. I mean, I still tell *you* and *then* I write it down in
my little journal.

*(Bruce looks up at him. Pause.)*

BRUCE *(Gently, a bit guiltily)*: What. *(Meaning "What's the
matter?")*
JONATHAN *(A beat; quietly)*: Nothing.

*(Jonathan and Bruce paint and write for a long beat.)*

Say hi for me.

*(Bruce doesn't respond.)*

Bruce? Say hi for—
BRUCE: Yeah.

*(Pause.)*

JONATHAN: What are you mad at *me* for?
BRUCE: Who's mad?!
JONATHAN: What are you mad at *me* for, *you're* the one who's
always writing to fucking Paula, you never talk to *me*
anymore . . .
BRUCE *(Over "anymore")*: Well, aren't we sick of each other
yet?, traveling around for five weeks?
JONATHAN: Are we? Gee. I guess we are. Gee, I—
YAKOV *(Off)*: HEY!! I don't believe you boys!

*(Jonathan and Bruce shoot their sights toward the direction
of the voice.)*

JONATHAN: Shit. It *is* Yakov . . .

*(In a beat, Yakov approaches from the direction in which he ran. He is drinking from a canteen. He smiles always, but his tone is mocking, disingenuous.)*

YAKOV: Are you deaf?

BRUCE: Me?

YAKOV: Are you *stupid*?

BRUCE: Huh?

YAKOV: I told you to get up before. Didn't you see me when I ran by?

BRUCE: Uh-huh.

YAKOV: I told you to get *up*, back to work.

BRUCE: I thought you were kidding.

YAKOV: Why would I be kidding? You've come here to work?, or you've come here to play? *(To Jonathan)* And what are *you* doing?

JONATHAN: Taking a break.

YAKOV: Oh. Tired?

JONATHAN *(Tentatively)*: Yes.

YAKOV: You've been picking for two hours and you're tired?

JONATHAN: Since 8:30. It's almost twelve.

YAKOV: You're breaking my heart. I've been keeping an eye on you boys. A little rest here, a little break there . . . What a spectacle you boys are. This is not Miami Beach, I hate to break it to you.

*(Yakov takes a long swig from his canteen, the water cascades down his neck and chest. He hands it to Jonathan.)*

JONATHAN *(Surprised; as he takes it)*: Thanks.

*(Bruce moves closer in anticipation; Jonathan tries to sip from it.)*

It's empty.

YAKOV *(Takes back the canteen)*: Oh, what a shame. *(Clicks his tongue)* I feel sorry for you boys. Brooklyn boys. So pale. So delicate. Hands like pampered little girls'. I cringe for you when I see you working in the orchard. Slow-motion photography. Not even lunchtime and you're ready for your nap. Look at *you* and look at *me*: to think that we all, in the eyes of the world, we are all Jewish men. *(He touches his crotch lasciviously)* Laughable. You don't know what hard work *is*, my friends . . . Boys . . . You American *children*. Your mommies and daddies send you over on jets, for what? To *edu*cate you? No, I'm *ask*ing you. To turn you into good little Zionists, what? Cultural exchange? What is the fascination? I don't understand. This is, what, an alternative to summer camp for you? Arts and crafts? I see you have your little sketchbook. *(Reaches for it; Jonathan resists)* Please. *(Jonathan hesitates, then gives it to Yakov, who looks through it)* Oh, so you are a good little artist. Look at that: the orchard! I see! *(Flips pages; a tad mocking)* Our cows, yes! Very good! Look at that: the Administration Building. Very talented. *(Returns the book to Jonathan)* This is my *life*, you know, this is my *home*. We kibbutzniks are not here for your entertainment. This is not a country club for rich Jewish children. I am not the boy who cleans the pool and changes your linens.

JONATHAN: I'm not "rich."

YAKOV: You're not? Forgive me. I don't mean rich. I mean . . . spoiled. Yes. Safe. You see, we go on in this fashion long after you fly home on your 747s. We remain. We are just an outing for you. Something to snap pictures of. This is not kibbutz-Disneyland where you ride the amusements and go home smiling. You have to participate. On our terms. You are our guests. But you are the kind who expect only to be served and never rise to clean the dishes.

JONATHAN: I washed the dishes last night.

YAKOV: So you did. You know what I mean. You aren't ignorant. What do you know of survival? What do you know of death? In the Six Day War, seventeen years old, I fought. How old are you?

JONATHAN *(Ashamed)*: That age.

YAKOV *(Laughs, then)*: And where were *you* in '67? Dragging yourself off to Hebrew lessons when you'd've rather been playing baseball? I was fighting for your right to exist. *(Pause. He touches Jonathan's face strangely, menacingly, sexually. A beat)* Back to work, boys.

*(He starts to go off, snatching a peach from the basket as he goes. Jonathan touches his cheek and looks at his fingers, as if he's checking for blood. He's shaken by the encounter. To dispel the tension, Bruce touches Jonathan's face in a lame attempt at a joke.)*

BRUCE: "Back to work, boys . . ."

*(Jonathan is not amused; he pushes Bruce's hand away.)*

JONATHAN: Fuck *you*, Bruce!

BRUCE *(Now also very upset)*: Well, fuck *you*!

*(In a flash, they're pushing and punching each other furiously. It's very heated and very quick. In the midst of the skirmish, Jonathan violently grabs Bruce's letter.)*

Jonathan! Jonathan, give me . . . Give it back!

*(Jonathan crumples the letter and throws it to the ground. They separate, out of breath, their adrenaline rushing wildly. Bruce retrieves the balled-up letter and smooths it out. Jonathan watches him for a beat.)*

JONATHAN: Bruce? Brucie? I'm sorry, Bruce . . .

*(Bruce ignores him as he gathers his things.)*

Bruce?

*(Bruce starts to go, walking past him; Jonathan reaches for his friend's shoulder.)*

Hey . . .

*(Bruce evades Jonathan's touch. Jonathan watches him exit. He watches him walk farther into the distance, then calls to him at the top of his lungs.)*

Brucie?!

*(Fade out.)*

# MISADVENTURE

*Misadventure* received its premiere in March 2000 at the Humana Festival of New American Plays at Actors Theatre of Louisville (Jon Jory, Producing Director) in Louisville, Kentucky, as a part of the "dramatic anthology" *Back Story*, based on characters created by Joan Ackerman. It was directed by Meredith McDonough. The set design was by Paul Owen, lighting was by Greg Sullivan, sound was by Martin R. Desjardins and costumes were by Kevin McLeod. The dramaturgs were Amy Wegener and Michael Bigelow Dixon and the stage manager was Amber D. Martin. Ainsley was played by Kimberly Megna and Ethan was played by Cary Calebs.

*The parking lot of the Danville, New Hampshire, police station. She's fuming. He's sheepish. It's cold.*

AINSLEY: Get in the car.

ETHAN *(Refusing)*: Un-uh.

AINSLEY: Get. In. The. Car.

ETHAN: No way.

AINSLEY: Ethan! Get in the car!

ETHAN: I refuse to get in the car when you're like this.

AINSLEY: Like what?

ETHAN: You're mad at me.

AINSLEY: I am not mad at you.

ETHAN: Yes you are; I can tell: your nostrils are doing that thing.

AINSLEY: What thing?

ETHAN: You know, they kinda . . . *(Demonstrates by flaring his nostrils)*

AINSLEY: GETINTHECAR!

ETHAN: I'm not getting in any car with you at the wheel when you're like this. What if you lose control and crash into a tree or something?

AINSLEY: I'm not gonna lose control.

ETHAN: How do you know? You might get this uncontrollable urge to smack me repeatedly and then what?

AINSLEY: I am not gonna smack you! Get in the car!

ETHAN: I've had enough trauma for one evening, thank you.

AINSLEY: *You've* had enough trauma!

ETHAN: Yes! The stigma of incarceration will haunt me for years.

AINSLEY *(Softly)*: Get in the car.

111

*(He shakes his head no.)*

Ethan, I am too tired and too pissed-off—

ETHAN: Ah-ha! *(Because she let her anger slip)*

AINSLEY *(Continuous)*: —to be having this argument with you in a police station parking lot in Nowhere, New Hampshire, in the middle of a freezing night. I'm cold and I want to go home.

ETHAN: I like the cold; the cold feels good. It's sobering me up. I feel more awake than I've ever felt in my life.

AINSLEY: What were you thinking?! What in the world were you thinking?!

ETHAN: I don't know.

AINSLEY: You don't *know*? Were you trying to *kill* yourself? Huh? *Were* you? *(He shrugs)* Were you looking to get yourself *killed*?

ETHAN: No. I don't know. Maybe.

AINSLEY: Maybe?! MAYBE?!

ETHAN: I don't know, I said.

AINSLEY: You selfish boy! You stupid selfish boy!

ETHAN: Good. Let it out. I'm glad we're talking now; it's much better than that nostril thing.

AINSLEY: How DARE you be reckless with your life! How DARE you!

ETHAN: Shhh! You're disturbing the peace. You want them to throw both of us in jail?

AINSLEY: What's my life worth if you trash yours? Huh? Have you thought about that?!! I'll have to live the next seventy-five years haunted every goddamn day by your pimply ghostly self! We're not just sibs, you stupid moron, we're soulmates! Don't you know that by now?!

ETHAN *(Childlike, surprised by the depth of her rage, he nods; a beat, then softly)*: I'm sorry.

AINSLEY: You drink yourself sick and go hitching on the interstate?! Are you crazy?! Have I taught you nothing?!

ETHAN: Hey. A. I said I was sorry.

AINSLEY: Never mind being drunk and weaving on the shoulder with cars and trucks whizzing by at eighty miles an hour. Never mind that. What if a crazy person stopped to picked you up—a Jeffrey Dahmer-type or something—

ETHAN *(Amused)*: What?!

AINSLEY: —and took you away so you were never heard from again! Some Boy Scouts would come across your jaw bone one day in the woods. It's a good thing the cops picked you up and threw you in jail. You could've been road kill.

ETHAN: You're nuts, you know that? You've been watching too much television!

AINSLEY: Don't mock me. There ARE crazy people out there, you know, they're not just CREATED by the media. They exist! There are truly bad and sick people out there in the world who want nothing more than to destroy other people's happiness. *(He cracks up)* Stop laughing! STOP IT!! It isn't funny! You scared me, Ethan! You scared me to death!!

*(She throws punches at him, he protects his head with his hands, laughing until she really hurts him.)*

ETHAN: Oww!

*(She stops. Silence.)*

That hurt.

AINSLEY: Good.

ETHAN: I can explain.

AINSLEY: Nothing you could possibly say . . .

ETHAN: Aren't you even gonna give me my due process? Aren't you?

AINSLEY: I don't see why I should.

ETHAN: I'm just a kid you know.

AINSLEY: Oh God. Is that your excuse? Is that your pissant excuse?!

ETHAN: Kids are *supposed* to act out and do reckless things. Right? If not while I'm young, when? When I'm old? When I'm forty?

AINSLEY: The key is surviving long enough to attain wisdom.

ETHAN: Okay, so I survived.

AINSLEY: You're not a cat, though, Ethan; that's what worries me: you only get one shot and you came awfully close this time . . .

ETHAN: Okay, so let's chalk it up to the folly of youth. Okay? I've learned my lesson: I drank a whole lot of really shitty bourbon with some asshole I don't even like whose approval I inexplicably crave and blew Pizza Hut pizza all down my front and onto my brand new running shoes. Don't you think I'm humiliated enough? I just *bought* these shoes. Like a week ago.

AINSLEY: If you'd killed yourself! . . . If you'd gotten yourself killed for some stupid, peer-pressure, macho, adolescent, alcoholic misadventure . . . If I'd lost you 'cause of it . . . If I'd *lost* you . . .

*(She finally lets herself weep; she turns away from him. He's impressed. Silence.)*

Pizza Hut, huh. No wonder you smell like a dairy farmer.

ETHAN: I can't even smell it anymore.

AINSLEY: Trust me.

ETHAN: Oh, yeah, why should I trust you?

AINSLEY: Because you'd better. Because if you don't trust me, brother, you are a goner. You are toast. *(A beat)* Now get in the car.

ETHAN: Still mad at me?

AINSLEY *(Smiling)*: Get in the fucking car?

ETHAN *(Smiles; a beat; as he gets into the car)*: Can we stop somewhere to get something to eat? I'm starving.

AINSLEY: We'll see. Phew. You stink.

*(She starts the car.)*

# ZIMMER

A PLAY IN ONE ACT FOR ONE ACTOR

*Zimmer* was commissioned and first presented by the Jewish Repertory Theatre (Ran Avni, Artistic Director; Edward M. Cohen, Artistic Associate) in New York City, on February 24, 1987. It was directed by Michael Arabian and performed by Joe Urla.

AUTHOR'S NOTE

The actor portraying the many characters depicted in this play should not resort to caricature, but instead capture the essence of the various men and women. The rapid transitions should have the effect of quick cutting used in film, and can be accomplished with deft lighting and a minimum of props. Think of this piece as a stage documentary of the fictional life of Ira Zimmer.

*Zimmer, a thirty-two-year-old man, in the record store where he works, speaking to a teenage girl.*

ZIMMER: Good album. Excuse me. Good album. Good choice. You should get it. You got any other Doors? Then get it. It's their first. It's good. It's got all their best stuff, like a "best-of." "Light My Fire," "The End." You should get it. I know I work here and everything, but if you want my advice, you should go ahead and get it, if you're gonna get any Doors at *all* . . . I mean like an intro*duc*tory thing. To *have*. If you like '60s music. If you like '60s music . . . Do you? I mean do you have an older brother or something? Yeah? How old is she? Nine*teen*? How old are *you*? I don't know, I thought you were in your twenties at least. Yeah. You're welcome. But if you've got an older sister who's nine*teen* . . . you were born in what, '65, '66? No wait, how can that be? '69? You were born in '69? I was at *Wood*stock in '69. I was in Woodstock and you were in Pampers, I don't believe it. '69? God I'm getting old. I could be arrested in some states for just *talk*ing to you. No. Why, how old do you think I am? How old. Guess. Oh, come on, do I look forty? I know I said I was old, but do I look *forty*? Of course not. I've still got my hair. Guys by the time they're forty . . . So you're, what, eighteen? Ah. Seventeen and a half. Whew. *(Smiles to himself)* Nothing. Just smiling. So if you're seventeen and a half . . . let's see, I'm less than twice your age. No, not thirty-six. Less than twice your age. If you're seventeen and a half, and I'm *less than* twice your age, how old am I? No, come back. What's the matter? 'Who's giving you a math lesson? Nobody's giving you a math lesson, we're talking. Okay? Okay? I'm thirty-two. Almost thirty-three. Yeah, that's less than twice your age. Thirty-two. Jesus, isn't that unbelievable. To me it is, to me it's *unbe*-lievable. Thirty-two years old . . . *(Shudders, sighs, sadly)* Anyway, this album. This album is a must if you're start-ing a '60s collection. I mean if you *were*. They were good, The Doors, in the beginning, really good, really special. Great sound. Ahead of their time. When they first came out . . . Yeah, he died. Like twenty-something. Can you imagine Jim Morrison alive today? Jim Morrison in his forties? Never. If he were alive today, he would've been dead by now. *(A beat. Sings, à la Morrison a song such as "The End")*

*(Lights shift. A beat.)*

*(To the audience)* Call me Zimmer. Z-I-double-M-E-R. My first name is Ira, but no one calls me Ira. Only peo-ple who don't know me very well call me Ira. My *moth*er did and my father did. And my sister and my grand-mother. My sister *still* calls me Ira, *when* she calls me.

*(A beat.)*

ZIMMER'S SISTER *(While breastfeeding)*: I look at my kids, Ira, and I see you. Look at Gregory. Don't you see you? I do. I'm old enough to remember, you know. I remember when Mommy and Daddy brought you home in the Olds. I waited outside with Bubba on Ocean Avenue, watching the traffic, waiting for Daddy's car. The burgundy Olds. I loved that car. It smelled like French's mustard 'cause of that picnic it spilled. I sat on her lap watching every sin-gle car. There it was, turning the corner of Avenue W. Bubba held my hand but I was jumping up and down. I got my baby brother! I got my baby brother! This kvetchy

118

pink roast beef in a blue fluffy blanket. Daddy picked me up so I could see you. Mommy couldn't bend. I remember everything. I have memories from the *crib* practically. *(Her baby nibbles on her)* Oww, easy, Gregory. That's Mommy's nipple. You *like* Mommy's nipple. He gets so carried away.

*(A beat.)*

THE ACTOR *(Speaking as himself, to the audience)*: Ira Mitchell Zimmer was born three weeks prematurely, on August 22, 1954, in Monticello, New York. Zimmer's mother's water broke while playing mah-jongg at Katzen's Bungalow Colony. Zimmer's parents grew up in East Flatbush within five blocks of one another and attended Samuel J. Tilden High School. They knew each other by sight but never spoke. Years later, Zimmer's mother would enjoy pointing to the photo of the Radio Club in her high school yearbook in which Red Zimmer is in the last row, second from the right, and Estelle is in the third row, dead center, looking just like Linda Darnell, the movie star. Red Zimmer joined the marines but missed participating in the Normandy invasion when he got drunk during a weekend leave, stumbled, and badly shattered several metatarsal bones in his left foot. He was sent home, where he never revealed the true nature of his wartime injury. Back in Brooklyn, in uniform and on crutches, Zimmer's father was treated like a hero. His family took him out to eat at Lundy's to celebrate his return, where he ran into the girl from high school who looked like Linda Darnell. Struck by the girl's beauty and, playing off her sympathy, he asked her out. They dated regularly for over a year. At the same time, Red was having sex with an Irish girl named Peggy every Thursday afternoon in her Stuyvestant Town apartment, following Red's whirlpool therapy for his injured foot.

Caught up in the euphoria after the Japanese surrender, Red drunkenly asked Estelle to marry him. They honeymooned at Niagara Falls during a blizzard and couldn't see a thing. Estelle suffered a miscarriage on New Year's Eve 1948, but went on to have two children, Carol Ann, born May 10, 1949, and Ira Mitchell, whose birth interrupted a mah-jongg game five years later. Zimmer's grandmother:

*(A beat.)*

ZIMMER'S GRANDMOTHER *(While unwrapping a candy)*: I remember your *bris*. The screams through the house. The blood. So much blood. Your poor little *schvantz*, clipped like a chicken at the butcher's. What blood! Your cousin Iris threw up. She was too young. I told them so. Too much excitement. The wine, the flashbulbs. The gefilte fish. The blood.

*(A beat.)*

ZIMMER, AGE FIVE *(Crying)*: I made him bleed, Mommy! This boy Richie! I made him bleed! We were in the pool and I bunked him! I bunked his face and his nose started bleeding! He cried! 'Cause of me! I bunked him! With my elbow! I'm sorry! The counselor Mark made us get out of the pool! We had to stop playing in the water! Richie's blood got in the water and everybody had to get out! 'Cause of me! There was red in the water!

*(A beat.)*

THE ACTOR: Richie Feldman and Zimmer soon became best friends. Richie was small, fat and seamy. Brooklyn's answer to Jack Ruby. He compulsively chewed on his knuckles until they were raw and bloody. His parents sent him to a doctor who wrapped gauze around his thumbs. When Richie chewed *through* the gauze to get to his skin, the doctor brushed Mercurochrome on his knuckles so that when Richie chewed on himself, his tongue would sting and his lips would turn orange. Richie masturbated in math class. His classmates got used to the sound of his fist rhythmically smacking the metal underside of his desk during quizzes. Richie had a sister named Bonnie who invented anorexia in the early '60s. His mother, a recluse, remained unseen by friends for years. She was a muffled voice demanding quiet from the next room, a disembodied hand serving milk and Mallomars through a darkened doorway. His father sold Israel bonds.

*(A beat.)*

ZIMMER, AGE EIGHT *(During an air-raid drill)*: *Take cover! (Covers his head, gets under his school desk giggling, playing with Richie)* Oh no! It's the end of the world! *(Makes exploding sounds)* We're all gonna die, Richie!, we're all gonna die! *(More sounds)* Shh, shh. She's coming. Shh. *(Giggles nervously as the teacher approaches. A beat. To the teacher)* Nothing. We were just—I know. I know this is serious. *(Shrugs)* 'Cause it could happen. Khrushchev could press the button and bomb Brooklyn, and then President Kennedy would have to push *his* button and bomb Moscow. And then we'd all be dead, the whole world. But what I don't understand is what difference does it make if we're quiet if we're gonna die anyway? So what if we laugh? It's not like the Russians'll *hear* us. I mean, they know we're here, it's not like we'll be giving ourselves away. Okay, we'll be quiet. We'll be quiet.

*(A beat. Zimmer watches as the teacher walks away. He looks at Richie and cracks up, then makes a final exploding sound. A beat.)*

THE ACTOR (*Reading a composition*): "P.S. 254, Class 4-209, November 26, 1963. *The Saddest Day of My Life*, by Ira Zimmer. Friday, November 22nd, nineteen hundred and sixty-three A.D., was the saddest day of my life. John Fitzgerald Kennedy, the youngest president of the United States of America, was assassinated in Dallas, Texas.

"They let us out of school early but everyone was sad. When I got to our building, all the mothers were outside. Many of them were crying. Nobody could believe that John F. Kennedy was dead and that Vice President Lyndon B. Johnson was now the thirty-sixth president of the United States.

"John F. Kennedy was so young and healthy. Who would ever have thought that he would die before the older Mr. Johnson?

"John F. Kennedy was like an uncle or a father you could be really proud of. He was smart, funny and good-looking, with a beautiful wife of French origin and two cute children, Caroline and John Jr., also known as John-John. John F. Kennedy made people feel good about the future. Now he is no more. I wish I could wake up and find out that the saddest day of my life was something I dreamt, but I don't think so because I believe that I am awake."

*(A beat.)*

ZIMMER (*To the audience*): When strangers call me Ira, it takes me a second to realize that they're talking to me. I don't correct them. I don't say: "Call me Zimmer" to just anyone. All my teachers called me Ira. Mr. Giordano, who I had for English in the tenth grade, called me Zimmer, but then he used to turn me on in his van in the teachers' parking lot, and we'd quote from Dylan and Ginsberg. He called me Zimmer but I never called him anything. My bar mitzvah teacher, Mr. Klein, he called me Yitzak.

*(A beat.)*

MR. KLEIN: No, no, no. Yitzak. Will you never get this right?
I'm wasting my breath on you. I tell you, day after day:
practice! Play your record and practice, but you don't listen. How do you expect to get through your bar mitzvah?
A miracle? No. No miracles for spoiled boys. This is very
funny to you. Laugh, go ahead, laugh. Get used to the
sound. There'll be a lot of laughter when you get up in
*shul* to recite your *haftorah* and nothing comes out of
your mouth! For thousands of years Jewish boys have
been able to do it except you. How does it feel? Hmm?
What is so important? Tell me: what is so important,
more important than learning your *haftorah*? What?
Baseball? Beatles? Rock and roll? You may as well get up
there and *announce,* announce to the congregation:
"I have nothing but contempt for each and every one of
you!" *(Begins to cough)* Oh, you are an unworthy boy.
Unworthy of manhood. Unworthy of living the kind of
life you live. So free. So spoiled. You're no better than my
son, may he rest in peace. I thought you were different.
You started with such promise. A nice face. A sweet
voice. You have the brains. But already you're lost! Lost,
and so young, so young. *(Coughing gets worse; breathing
becomes difficult)* I'm old. I'm old and it's hot, and there's
plenty of things I'd rather be doing than eating my
*kishkas* out over a spoiled boy in a hot room. You're a
*shanda.* For *this* six million died?! So a spoiled boy in
Brooklyn should make a mockery?! For *this*?! *(Stricken,
he realizes he's having a heart attack)* Oh, my God . . .
Yitzak . . . Ira . . . get help . . . please . . . don't stand there,
help me! God will punish you!

*(He falls. A beat. Zimmer, twelve years old, watches in hor-
ror and fascination. A beat.)*

THE ACTOR: Summer, 1969. Zimmer is a junior counselor at Camp Shalom in Upstate New York. On the night of August 15th, Richie Feldman shows up and coerces Zimmer into going AWOL and coming with him to the Woodstock Music and Art Fair. The following night, while Richie and Zimmer revel in the mud and the music, Zimmer's parents are in Long Island, attending the wedding of his cousin, Iris. While driving home from Leonard's of Great Neck, Zimmer's father, feeling the effects of four whiskey sours, plus a champagne toast to the bride and groom, loses control of his Dodge Polara and hits a freezer truck carrying Dolly Madison ice cream. Zimmer's mother is killed instantly. The Van Wyck Expressway is shut down for six and a half hours, causing massive delays. The melted ice cream alone creates a terrible nuisance. Zimmer's father suffers multiple fractures and bruises, and is hospitalized way the hell out in Jamaica, Queens. Broken and depressed like Montgomery Clift, Zimmer's father returns to work at his liquor store in early November, keeping long hours to avoid going home. At 1:30 on the morning of Thanksgiving Day, a thirteen-year-old black kid panics during a holdup and Zimmer's father is shot and killed. On January 2, 1970, cousin Iris's marriage is annulled.

*(A beat.)*

ZIMMER: John F. Kennedy was in it, I remember *that*. We was walking around and talking and everything, but most of his head was missing. I knew it was John F. Kennedy, though. You know how it is in dreams?, when you *know* something even though it doesn't look absolutely like what you know it's supposed to be? Like, this man, John F. Kennedy, could very well have been my father, who right around this time was murdered also, but in the dream the man is definitely John F. Kennedy. Maybe he was like an actor playing my father. Anyway, he was really pretty cheerful, considering. He was tan and everything. Smiling. I wondered how he could be in such good spirits, smiling and everything, even though he'd been dead for something like five years at this point and his brain was mostly blown away. So I went up and asked him. He was in our kitchen. Of our old house, before my mother died and then my father, before me and my sister had to move in with my grandmother. Oh, *I* remember now: there were these workmen in the kitchen in my dream, hacking away at the walls. There was plaster dust everywhere. They were destroying my mother's kitchen! And there were these three big, elderly black women in flowered housedresses. Three of them, cooing and clucking at one another like a trio of pigeons. I couldn't understand what they were saying. But one of them, she had her glasses hanging on a string around her neck, and she picked them up and looked at me and smiled sympathetically. For some reason, I decided these three black women were like the eternal custodians of our old apartment. It was their job to get it ready for the next tenants, just as they'd done for centuries. I felt very sad, in the dream. And then it was like John F. Kennedy all of a sudden beamed up in the kitchen, wearing his gray, presidential-looking suit, and got himself a beer. *Then* I went up to him and said, "Excuse me, Mr. President, but I can't believe how well you look." "Thank you, Zimmer," he said. He called me "Zimmer"! "I mean, except for the back of your head, you look like you always did. If you didn't turn around, nobody could tell you were dead." And he said, "That's very reassuring. If I could get away with not appearing dead, I'd be a very happy man, indeed." Well, there was every indication that the famous Kennedy wit was in no way impaired by the loss of brain tissue. I was relieved that death doesn't have to destroy one's sense of humor. He made some crack about The

Single Bullet Theory—had me in stitches. I couldn't believe that I was standing in my own kitchen with this man who'd meant so much to me my entire life. I tried to tell him, but I couldn't. I started crying. Then he put his arm around me. John F. Kennedy, he had his arm around me. "It's not so bad, Zimmer," he said. "Nothing is lost," he said, "nothing is lost."

*(A beat.)*

ZIMMER, AGE FIFTEEN *(Excitedly)*: Okay, Richie, listen. *(A beat; listening to a record)* See?! You hear that?! "I buried Paul." That's what John is saying: "I buried Paul." Shit, I'm getting chills. Look at the *Sgt. Pepper* cover. Look. I mean, come on, what is that? The flowers and the people standing around in the dirt? I mean, where do people stand around in the dirt with flowers all around? A funeral. It's a funeral. I'm not saying it *is* a funeral, I'm saying it *represents* a funeral. It represents Paul's funeral. Laugh all you like, Richie, Paul is dead. The Beatles are finished. God, I'm so depressed. The *Beat*les, Richie. So what if he's not your favorite Beatle? He's not *my* favorite Beatle, either, but still: Paul McCartney, the cute Beatle. It's the end of an era, Richie. They're dropping clues everywhere! "A Day in the Life"?—John says: "He blew his mind out in a car," right? "Don't Pass Me By"?—Ringo sings: "You were in a car crash and you lost your hair." Paul was killed in a car crash and they didn't want the world to know because it would be too much. I mean, could you imagine the hysteria? You saw what Beatlemania was like, can you imagine *dead* Beatlemania? Girls would be killing themselves all over the world! So, they hired this guy who kinda *looked* like Paul, and gave him plastic surgery, and taught him how to play leftie. I feel so dumb. I never suspected. Wait, the *Abbey Road* cover: check out the car. What the license plate say? Un-uh, not 2-8-I-F,

28 IF. Paul would've been twenty-eight *if* he were alive. Wow, right? Huh? Huh? Unbelievable. Okay, now listen to the end of "I Am the Walrus" played backwards.

*(A beat.)*

THE ACTOR: 1971. A poem by Zimmer is published in his high school literary magazine. *(Reads, tongue in cheek)* The War in My Head, by Ira Zimmer:

> There's this war that's raging in my head,
> in black-and-white, nonstop.
> Huntley and Brinkley invaded my brain
> and don't shut up, they won't shut up.
> See, this war in my head
> kills my sleep
> poisons my dreams
> drugs my days.
> See, my head aches with all these
> noisy dead men crying
> but there ain't no Paris peace talks
> for this war in my head.
> No relief, no aspirin, no secretaries of state.
> No, I don't have to go to no Vietnam
> by army plane and boat and helicopter
> 'cause there's this war, see, right here in my head
> that kills my sleep and poisons my days.
> And what it's done to my dreams, man,
> it just ain't fair.
> No, it ain't fair.

*(A beat.)*

ZIMMER'S SISTER *(While breastfeeding)*: You and me, we're very different, Ira, you *know* that. *You* know that and *I* know that. I think I was put on this earth to have babies. That's what I do best. It's such a complete and total turn-on for me, I can't tell you. Being pregnant, nursing. I could come right now, I swear. *(Giggles)* If only you could find yourself a girl. I know, I know, I sound like your mother. Mommy would never even've said that to you. But a girl, Ira. You gotta try to hold onto something for a change. You never even tried. *Love,* Ira. Babies.

*(A beat.)*

ZIMMER, AGE NINETEEN *(On the telephone)*: Hello, is Wendy there? Tell her Zimmer. Zimmer. Ira, yeah. Hi. How come, is she sick? Look, I'm sure if you told her I was on the phone . . . Could you? Could you just tell her it's me, she won't mind getting out of bed, I promise. Ask her. Give her the choice. I'm *not* being smart, Mrs. Siegerman . . . Thank you. *(To himself)* Jesus . . . *(Pause)* You sure your mother doesn't work for the S.S.? Hi. So what happened?, you were supposed to meet me at the Fillmore, you okay? You sure? You sound funny. Yeah, you do. So where were you? Yeah, I *was* worried, what do you think? I mean, it wasn't *pleasant* standing there by myself, thinking I was seeing you every ten seconds. There are so many Wendy clones with light brown frizzy hair, you would not believe it. I kept on asking these freaks to hold my place in line so I could call my grandmother to see if you'd called to say you were late or dead or something. I decided you *were* dead. Murdered on the QB. I am *not* morbid. What did you *think* I'd think when you stand me up like that?! I mean, Wendy, come on!, how was I supposed to know you didn't feel like it? We had so much fun when we waited for Crosby, Stills, Nash and Young, didn't we? Well? Why not The Who? If you didn't really like them . . . Don't you even want to know if I got us tickets? Yeah, I did. Don't you want to know *where*? Fifth row. So what's the matter? Don't tell me nothing. What did I do, you're mad at me. Yes you are, why else are you acting so weird? Okay!, so you don't feel well!, what's the matter with you!? *(A beat; nervous smile)* Yeah, right. *(Long pause; quietly)* Right there in his office he did it? Did it hurt? *(Pause)* Why didn't you tell me? I mean, don't you think you should've told me? I mean, I got you into this, you could've *told* me ... No wonder your mother was so ... *(A beat)* You didn't tell her it was me? It *was* me, wasn't it? I mean, I *was* the one, wasn't I? I mean, don't I even get credit for *that*? I mean, shit, Wendy, why the fuck didn't you tell me in the first place? You knew all this time and you knew what you were gonna *do* about it and you never even *told* me?! What *am* I to you anyway? *(Pause)* I'm gonna let you go now. Uh, look, don't worry about the ticket. I'll get Richie or somebody to come with me. So, take it easy, I hope you feel better. Yeah. 'Bye.

*(A beat.)*

THE ACTOR: Zimmer drops out of Brooklyn College after one semester and travels cross-country with Richie Feldman. In Las Vegas, Richie tries to persuade Zimmer to share a prostitute with him. Zimmer refuses, they argue, and split up. Zimmer uses all of his pocket money to purchase a Trailways bus ticket. Once back at his grandmother's house in Brooklyn, Zimmer stays in his room for five months.

*(A beat. Zimmer, age twenty, headphones on, smoking a joint, singing a few bars of a song like Bob Dylan's "Like a Rolling Stone" loudly and off key. A beat.)*

ZIMMER'S SISTER: I'm very disappointed in you, Ira, if you want to know the truth. I had high aspirations for you. Ever since you were a little boy. You had such patience.

Playing by yourself, making the most beautiful pictures, for hours at a time. You were so quiet, Mommy was always asking if you were okay. You were so fucking talented. You were! I'm not saying I'm jealous, I'm saying you were amazing! There were so *many* things you could do! The music and the art! The poetry in the school magazine! Where did that *come* from, Ira?, the poetry! I thought you'd've been a famous *some*thing by now. Thirty-two years old. A famous record producer or something. A David Geffen. I thought you'd've been doing something special with your life. What the hell happened? You were supposed to put the Zimmers on the map. We're not on any map, Ira, we should've been. We're not on any map.

*(A beat.)*

THE ACTOR: Between 1974 and 1980, Zimmer does the following: enrolls in a night course at Kingsborough Community College in Literature of the Fantastic: from *Lord of the Rings* to *Cat's Cradle*, but attends only four times; sells tie-dyed T-shirts at the Sunrise drive-in flea market for three summers; deals marijuana for eight months, and earns twenty-one thousand dollars; sells Amway products and successfully recruits his brother-in-law, who today is an Amway district supervisor; attends a series of Scientology seminars, where he meets Anita Santiago, a junior at NYU, with whom he has sex every Thursday night for ten months; sells car radios at Crazy Eddie; works in the Pop section of J & R Music World; is promoted to assistant floor manager of the Rock 'n' Roll department, where he can still be found Tuesday through Saturday. *(A beat)* On December 8, 1980, after the murder of John Lennon, Zimmer visits Richie Feldman at a drug rehabilitation clinic on the Lower East Side. Zimmer brings a cassette player, a selection of Beatles tapes, and a six-pack of Budweiser. It's their first meeting since going their separate ways in a Las Vegas parking lot seven years earlier. They play all of the tapes, some of them two and three times, drink all of the beer, and reminisce. Richie begins to rant incoherently . . . *(The Actor "becomes" Zimmer)* . . . Something about a bloody nose he says I gave him. I thought he was joking at first, and the next thing I knew, he hit me in the head with the cassette player. Richie ran out onto East 9th Street, where he was struck and killed by a gypsy cab.

*(A beat.)*

ZIMMER'S GRANDMOTHER *(While unwrapping a candy)*: It was the drugs. Once that Richie, that boy Richie, started you on the drugs, I could see you disappearing. Fading away. A ghost like all the rest. The smoke of those joints in your room. Constantly, constantly. It got so, my furniture smelled from it. My pillow. The milk in the Frigidaire. It became such a way of life, that even *I* didn't smell it anymore. Who knows, maybe I was stoned myself, breathing the same air all those years. That Richie . . . What could I do? An old lady all of a sudden raising two teenagers. The hair, the music, the craziness. What could I do? I ate my heart out from you. What did I know from joints and grass and all that *chazarai?* Uch . . . There *is* such a thing as being cursed, you know. My curse was to lose everything I had hope in. My brilliant grandson with the future. What happened to the future, *tateleh?*, what?

*(A beat. Fade up on Zimmer in the record store, as in the beginning of the play, singing the closing lyric of a song like "The End" by the Doors. A beat.)*

ZIMMER *(To the audience)*: I am Zimmer. I am "one who zims." I zim through life. I zim along the surface, the way a good skater zims across the ice. I zim, like the bullets that zim off of Superman's chest, like Hendrix would zim on his guitar. There is no meaning to the verb "to zim"; I give it meaning. *I* zim. I have zimmed, I will continue to zim. I lost Ira somewhere along the way. He just couldn't keep up with my zimming. *(Shrugs)* I zim.

*(Lights fade. Music: The Doors' "The End.")*

# SPACE

*Space* was commissioned and first presented by New Writers at the Westside in New York City, in June 1986. It was directed by Chris Silva. Man A was played by Dennis Boutsikaris and Man B was played by John Griesemer.

*Two men, A and B, in their mid-thirties. B's apartment, late at night, after eating, drinking and smoking dope.*

A *(Speaks very slowly)*: You're out there. In the middle of the desert. At night. And you turn off the headlights. And you're. The darkness. Like you're floating. In space. Like you're in space. You *feel* it. You *feel*. The nothingness. The, the. The *huge*ness. The utter. Vastness. Of space. And you'd think it should be quiet. Because it's so black. Because of all the nothingness. But, no. Then your ears. The motor is off. You turn off the motor and you hear. This buzz. This, this *symphony*. Of life. Of living things, you know? *(Pause)*

B: We never went to the desert, me and Nan.

A: Oh, it's elemental. It's. There's so much life like you're not even aware of out there. All that emptiness. All that seemingly empty space. *(Pause)*

B: I *wanted* to. She wasn't interested.

A: 'Cause the thing is. What makes it so elemental, the desert? Are the contradictions. You know what I mean?

B: Uh-huh.

A: The contradictions. Like the temperature. You're sweaty *and* cold. At the same time. What do you call it?

B: What.

A: At the same time.

B: Simultaneously?

A: Yes, but that's not the word.

B: Um . . .

A: That's not what I'm thinking of.

*(Pause.)*

B: Concurrently?

A: No . . .

B: Happening at the same time?

A: I can't think.

B: Anyway . . .

A: Anyway, the temperature. Paradoxes? Do I mean paradoxes?

B: Paradoxes?, yes.

A: Maybe. Maybe that's what I mean. Something and yet something else?, something that seemingly. Contradicts. The first thing?

B: Yeah . . .

A: Days. It could go above. The temperature could *surpass* a hundred, hundred and *ten* sometimes. At night. The temperature. Could drop sixty degrees easy. Plummet. The temperature plummets. The mercury. Way down.

B: I should've just taken off and gone by myself.

A: Wait: so, you're out there. In all this space. And this buzzing?

B *(Preoccupied, then testily)*: What?

A *(After a beat)*: Are you mad at me or something?

B: No.

A: I'm painting a picture for you. What it was like.

B: Go ahead.

A *(After a beat; meaning "What's the matter?")*: What.

B: Nothing. Tell me. Paint.

A *(After a beat, proceeding cautiously)*: There's this buzzing. This music. I mean it. It *is* like a symphony or something. These creatures. Crickets and insects. And. Creatures. Sounds. Coming. Emanating. Coming out of the air, almost. Yeah, it seems to come out of the air. Or up through the earth. Like the sand is, is. The earth's skin. And this sound. This electricity. Yeah, it's an *electrical* sound. This sound seeps out of the earth's pores. And you feel yourself hum with it. You feel the buzz of your own aura. Like your life-force has a sound, too. Just like the lizards and the crickets and the creatures and stuff. You know?

B: Yeah . . .

A: And the next thing that happens. The next thing you're *aware* of. And the thing is, we weren't even stoned yet. That's right, we weren't. On purpose. We wanted to be straight. At least in the beginning. So we could experience it, you know, unadulterated. So we could come to our own conclusions, you know?

B: Uh-huh.

A: Without drugs.

B: That's good.

A: You know? With*out* drugs. *Later* we got stoned. But in the beginning . . .

B: You were straight.

A: We were straight. That was a choice. A conscious decision. And I'm glad.

B: Uh-huh?

A: I'm very glad. *(A beat)* So what was I saying? *(Pause)*

B: The—

A: Oh! So, the next thing you notice. After the buzz. Your eyes. They adjust to the darkness. And you know what?

B: What?

A: It isn't dark at all. It's like almost blindingly lit up. The desert is. Illuminated. By the moon! I'm talking just like seconds into it. Once you adjust. A) the buzz. B) the brightness. You can see everything in sight! Mountains and bushes and cactuses. Cacti. And like lizards 'tween your toes. And clouds! You can see a couple of clouds! And the moon! It's true! The moon is like a silver hole in the sky lighting up everything in sight! And stars twinkle like they're special effects or something. It's unreal. It is unreal. And we take off our clothes. It's like Katie and I, we're Adam and Eve. And the desert is our garden. And then we did it.

B: Uh-huh.

A: Unbelievable.

B: I bet.

A: No, the feeling. This feeling of, of. Of nature. Of being a part of the cosmic buzz, you know? God. Amazing. *(Pause. Sadly)* We had such a great time out west. *(Pause)*

B: You want to sleep on the couch?

A: No, no.

B: It's no hassle. You *can*.

A: No, I'll go. I'll go home.

B: 'Cause I have to get up early.

A: I understand.

B: I'm temping.

A: I understand.

B: I've got to shlep all the way out to Long Island City.

A: I understand, really.

B: Some *furn*iture place.

A: I'll get out of your way.

B: 'Cause you're welcome to . . .

A *(Not budging)*: I'll go home.

B: I mean it.

*(A nods "I know." Pause.)*

Well, here we are. *(A beat)* Did you ever think we'd end up like this, you and me? *(A shakes his head)* Me neither. I thought I'd've been a father by now. Nan was making good money, we could've had a kid.

A: What is it with these women?

*(B shakes his head. After a beat:)*

I don't understand it. This trip out west. Things were never better.

B: I know, pal.

A: Everything had seemed to come together. But. At the same time. Everything was falling apart.

B: I know.

A: It's a paradox.

B: I'm really sorry. I really am.

A: Let's analyze this. *(B's heart sinks)* *I* felt we were never closer. *She* felt closed-in. That's what she told me. We were watching the sun rise and it's like she went cold on me. Like she shut off the juice.

B: You're gonna drive yourself nuts, you know that?

A: I should've known. I should've seen it coming. *(He smacks his own forehead)*

B: Hey!

A *(After a beat)*: We were. You know. While we were doing it? Katie was on top. Bouncing. Her hair blowing in the stars. Both of us breathing hard. Buzzing along with everything else. Sand crunching my back. The sweat and the goosebumps. Everything, in other words. Everything. I was watching Katie go. Bouncing. Her eyes closed. I was watching Katie. And over by her ear. In the sky. I saw it. We went to the desert to see Halley's Comet. And there it was. Katie wearing it like an earring. I didn't tell her. I didn't want to ruin it. Halley's Comet. I'm sure it was. This smudge. This nothing little white smudge. Halley's Comet. *(He shakes his head in disappointment. A beat)*

B: I'm getting you a pillow. You're sleeping on the couch.

*(B goes. A continues to shake his head.)*

# WOMEN IN MOTION

*Women in Motion* was commissioned and first presented by the Lucille Ball Festival for New Comedy (David Munnell, Artistic Director) in Jamestown, New York, on May 24, 1991. It was directed by Rand Foerster. Libby was played by Kathryn Rossetter and Monica was played by Carol McCann.

## SCENE 1

### On a Plane

*Libby and Monica, two single women in their thirties, vacationing together. The women have been drinking. Spirits are high. A friendly argument is in progress.*

LIBBY: But she's a prostitute!

MONICA: She's not a prostitute, she's, *you* know, a *call* girl.

LIBBY: That's not a call girl, Monica, a call girl doesn't hang out on Sunset Boulevard. That's a hooker. She's a hooker.

MONICA: But she's not *into* it. She's *new* at it.

LIBBY: He doesn't know that. Why would a guy who looked like that have to pick up a hooker in the first place?

MONICA: He was lost, remember?

LIBBY: Bullshit.

MONICA: He *was.* Don't you remember? That's why she got in with him.

LIBBY: Give me a break. A guy who looks like that, with the kind of money he had, he could have *any*body, why would he want a hooker from the streets?

MONICA: Because she was beautiful.

LIBBY: Uch, did you think she was beautiful?

MONICA: Yes!

LIBBY: With that awful wig? She wasn't beautiful.

MONICA: But that's the thing: he could *tell* that she was really beautiful.

LIBBY: Not when he picked her up in the car he couldn't. How could he? The girl she was *with* was more attractive.

MONICA: Did you think so? Uch, I didn't think so at all.

LIBBY: It didn't make any sense to me why he would go for *her.*

MONICA: God, Libby, where's your imagination? Where's your sense of romance?

LIBBY: I don't see what's so romantic about picking up a prostitute who could give you AIDS, and letting her live in your hotel room with you.

MONICA: Libby . . .

LIBBY: How did *he* know she wasn't a drug addict or something?

MONICA: What?!

LIBBY: She could've ripped him off or killed him or something.

MONICA: God, Libby, it's a *movie,* it's not real life.

LIBBY: I *know* it's a movie, Monica.

MONICA: Of *course* in real life you'd have to ask questions, but it's a *movie.*

LIBBY: I can't believe you saw it so many times. *How* many times did you see it?

MONICA: I don't even know anymore. I bought the tape for $14.99? I leave it in my VCR. Every night I watch a little bit before I go to sleep.

LIBBY: I don't be*lieve* you! *Every* night?

MONICA: So? Don't you look at a book sometimes before you go to sleep?

LIBBY: Yeah, but not the same book every night.

MONICA: It helps me fall asleep, okay? I *love* this movie. I can't believe you didn't love it.

LIBBY: Don't take it so personal; we're gonna be together the next five nights and six days, you shouldn't take it so personal.

MONICA: I'm not. *(A beat)* I'm sorry you didn't like it.

LIBBY: It's only a movie, you know . . .

MONICA: I know.

LIBBY: . . . it's not the end of the world.

MONICA: I know. *(A beat)* Maybe 'cause you saw it on a plane.

LIBBY: Monica, I wouldn't've liked it even if I saw it at Radio City.

MONICA: How could you tell if you liked something on a plane? You can't tell on a plane, these plastic things sticking in your ears, people keeping their shades up. Besides, they cut the best scene. The best scene she goes down on him, he's watching Lucy.

LIBBY: Which one?

MONICA: Which what?

LIBBY: Which Lucy?

MONICA: The one with the grapes.

LIBBY: Oh, yeah. *(She smiles)*

MONICA: Next time you come over, I'll play it.

LIBBY: I don't *want* to see it again.

MONICA: I'll play you the *scene* I'm talking about. It's a sexy scene. Don't you think he's sexy? *(Libby shrugs)* You *don't*? I can't believe you don't think he's sexy.

LIBBY: He's all right.

MONICA: All *right*? He's gorgeous.

LIBBY: He doesn't do it for me, Monica, what can I tell ya.

MONICA: Don't you think he's aged like really incredibly well?

LIBBY: That I agree with. I never liked his looks. He always looked so smoothed out, you know, like his face had something missing.

MONICA: Don't you think he looks a little like Mike?

LIBBY: Like *Mike*? Are you kidding?

MONICA: No?

LIBBY: He looks nothing like Mike.

MONICA: How can you say that? Mike is gorgeous.

LIBBY: Mike is very good *look*ing but he's not gorgeous. I wouldn't call Mike gorgeous. You always had this thing for Mike. I don't get it.

MONICA: Oh God, when he gets close to me to give me something to type? I feel like my heart is making so much noise he can hear me and I get embarrassed. I love the way he smells. Aramis he wears.

LIBBY: How do you know?

MONICA: My brother wears it. *(A beat)* What's his story do you think?

LIBBY: Mike?

MONICA: Yeah. You don't think he's *gay* or anything.

LIBBY: *Mike?* No.

MONICA: I mean, any man that dresses that good . . .

LIBBY: Mike is not gay.

MONICA: You sure?

LIBBY: I'm sure. Believe me, I'm sure.

MONICA: Uh-huh. *(A beat)* What's that mean?

LIBBY: What's what.

MONICA: What you just said. The way you said it, what do you mean?

LIBBY: Nothing.

MONICA: You said it like you know something.

LIBBY: Monica, will you stop analyzing everything I say and do?

MONICA: *Tell* me. How do *you* know so much about Mike? You've been in the office less than I have.

LIBBY: I don't know, I just know.

MONICA: Libby . . .

*(A beat.)*

LIBBY: He came on to me, okay.

MONICA: You're kidding me.

LIBBY: No.

MONICA: When?

LIBBY: Before the Christmas party.

MONICA: Be*fore?* Where?

LIBBY: By the Xerox.

MONICA: You're kidding me.

LIBBY: Un-uh.

MONICA: You were in the Xerox room with Mike?

LIBBY: Uh-huh.

MONICA: What were you doing?

LIBBY: Xeroxing.

MONICA: And he came in?

LIBBY: Uh-huh.

MONICA: Just the two of you?

LIBBY: Yeah. Well, Carmen was there, too. She was collating but she left.

MONICA: So it was just you and Mike?

LIBBY: Uh-huh.

MONICA: I'm dying. I can't believe you didn't tell me this.

LIBBY: I didn't want to upset you. I know you have this thing for Mike.

MONICA: You're right, you were smart, it's a good thing. So what happened?

LIBBY: The Xerox started eating paper.

MONICA: Yeah? So what you do?

LIBBY: We fixed it.

MONICA: You and Mike?

LIBBY: Uh-huh.

MONICA: Together?

LIBBY: Yeah. *You* know: I pulled out the thing, he pulled out the paper.

MONICA: And?

LIBBY: And he asked me what I was doing for vacation.

MONICA: He did? So what you tell him?

LIBBY: I told him I was going the Caribbean with *you.*

MONICA: Oh God, you told him you were going with *me?*

LIBBY: Christ, Monica, calm down.

MONICA: I'm sorry. So what he say?

LIBBY: He said, "Oh, that's nice."

MONICA: He did?

LIBBY: Something like that. And then he asked me what I was doing New Year's.

MONICA: You're kidding me.

LIBBY: No.

MONICA: Mike asked *you* what you were doing New Year's? You mean Mike isn't seeing anyone? Don't you think if

he asked you what you were doing New Year's that means
he was free?

LIBBY: I don't know, maybe he just wanted to know.

MONICA: Why would he want to know something like that?

LIBBY: Maybe he was just curious, I don't know. Do you want
me to tell you this or not?

MONICA: Yes yes yes, I'm sorry. So anyway go on. He asked
you what you were doing New Year's and . . .

LIBBY: I said we were flying home on the first.

MONICA: Yeah . . . ?

LIBBY: And he said, "That's too bad." He and Ed McCarthy
are throwing a party.

MONICA: Oh. Ed McCarthy from Accounting?

LIBBY: I guess.

MONICA: How come *I* didn't know about this party?

LIBBY: I don't know, I didn't either.

MONICA: Yeah, but he told *you*. He practically in*vited* you.

LIBBY: But I couldn't go. I was going here with you.

MONICA: Yeah, but nobody told *me*. How come nobody invited
*me*?

LIBBY: Monica, everybody knew you were going away. Nobody
invited me either. 'Cause they knew you and me were
going to the Caribbean. I knew I shouldn't've told you.

MONICA: I'm not upset. I'm not. This is very interesting. How
come nobody told me about this party?

LIBBY: I don't understand you. We're on our way to the Caribbean. What do *you* care about this stupid party?

MONICA: I don't. I'm only saying isn't this interesting. *(Libby
looks through a magazine. Pause)* I'm *glad* we're not gonna
be there, aren't you?

LIBBY: It doesn't matter to me one way or the other, Monica,
I don't care about the stupid party.

MONICA: I know, you're right. *(Pause)* Uh! I can't wait till we're
sitting in the sun, right?

LIBBY: I know. Me, neither.

MONICA: I cannot wait. *(Pause)*

LIBBY: Please, God, let there be sex.
MONICA: Amen.

*(They laugh.)*

## SCENE 2
### *At Poolside*

*The women, in bathing suits, on chaise lounge chairs. Monica is reading a romance novel. Libby, lying on her stomach with her bikini straps undone, is reading a magazine.*

MONICA: Can you believe this place?
LIBBY: Mmm.
MONICA: It's gorgeous. It's like paradise. Looks just like the brochure. Doesn't it?
LIBBY: Yeah.
MONICA: Not a cloud in the sky, the water . . . Can you believe that water? This place is totally unreal. When I saw the water in the brochure I thought: can't be, there *is* no such color, they made up a color like that. But can you believe that color?
LIBBY: Mmm. I know.

*(Pause.)*

MONICA: I'm *so* glad we did this. Aren't you?
LIBBY: Oh, yeah.
MONICA: Uch, can you imagine being in the city?
LIBBY: Yeah.
MONICA: The crowds and the cold and everything? Uch, if I had to spend another Christmas with my family . . . *(Pause)* I can't believe we just got here. I was just thinking to myself, isn't this funny? I feel like we've been here for

days. Don't you? Don't you feel like you've been here for days?

LIBBY: Mmm.

MONICA: I feel like we've been here a week. I feel so relaxed. I can't believe how relaxed I feel. *(A beat)* You should put some stuff on, you know. You're burning.

LIBBY: I am?

MONICA: You want me to?

LIBBY: I *put* some stuff on. I put 25.

MONICA: I know but you're burning anyway. I can tell with these sunglasses. You're turning pink. Your shoulders. They say if you sweat or swim . . . You want me to do it?

LIBBY: You mind?

MONICA: Not at all.

LIBBY: Thanks, it's in my thing.

*(Monica gets a bottle of sun block out of Libby's bag and applies the lotion.)*

MONICA: You have pretty skin.

LIBBY: Thank you.

MONICA: My back breaks out. *(A beat)* Wasn't lunch great?

LIBBY: It was all right.

MONICA: Just all right? Didn't you think it was delicious?

LIBBY: It was chicken salad with pineapple in it.

MONICA: Yeah, I know, I thought it was delicious. What an interesting combination. I'm gonna have to try that. Tropical chicken salad.

LIBBY: It was canned pineapple.

MONICA: That wasn't canned pineapple.

LIBBY: Yes it was. It was a ring. Like you get from Dole.

MONICA: Libby, that was not canned pineapple. This is the tropics. They *grow* pineapple here. What do they need to get it from cans for?

LIBBY: I'm telling you, mine had a piece of ring in it. Fresh pineapple doesn't come in rings, that much I know.

MONICA: So what if it was?

LIBBY: Was what?

MONICA: So what if it did come from a can? Does that mean it wasn't good?

LIBBY: All I'm saying, for what they charge you, they could at least give you fresh pineapple. That's all I'm saying.

*(Pause.)*

MONICA *(Quietly)*: I thought it was very good. *(A beat)* I suppose you didn't like the dessert either?

LIBBY: No, the dessert was good.

MONICA: Oh. Well.

*(Libby ties her bikini top and sits up.)*

LIBBY: Monica. Why must you take everything so personal?

MONICA: I don't.

LIBBY: Yes, you do. I tell you it was canned pineapple and you get all huffy with me.

MONICA: I do not get huffy.

LIBBY: Okay. Whatever you say.

*(Pause.)*

MONICA: I'm sorry you didn't like the chicken salad.

LIBBY: I said it was all right! I didn't say I didn't like it! It's not like you *made* it!

MONICA: I know.

LIBBY: It's really no big deal!

MONICA: Okay!

*(Long pause. Both resume reading.)*

We're not having a fight, are we?

LIBBY: Who said we're having a fight?

MONICA: I'm only asking.

LIBBY: No we are not having a fight.

MONICA: Good. I didn't think so. *(Pause)* I hate fights.

LIBBY: This isn't a fight.

MONICA: I know, I'm just saying. My parents used to fight all the time. It was horrible. The stupidest things they'd fight about. *(A beat)* Can we go dancing tonight please?


SCENE 3

*In the Bar of the Hotel*

*The women are seated at a table drinking daiquiris and watching other people dance. Dance music.*

LIBBY: Wait, look at *her.*

MONICA: Who?

LIBBY: The one with the hair.

MONICA: Oh God! *Look* at her! She looks like Ann-Margret or something. Can you believe men actually find that attractive?

LIBBY: *He* does.

MONICA: You think he's her husband?

LIBBY: No way, are you kidding?, they probably just met down here.

MONICA: Uch. Really? Look how she's letting him hold her.

LIBBY: I know.

MONICA: His hands are all over her.

LIBBY: Some guys get off on that. Public display.

MONICA: I think it's disgusting.

LIBBY: They probably already did it.

MONICA: You think?

LIBBY: Why not?

MONICA: I don't know. They're not even tan.

LIBBY: So?

MONICA: I mean, if they're not tan, they couldn't've been down here very long; how long could they have known each other?

LIBBY: Unless . . .

MONICA: What.

LIBBY: Unless they're in their room *do*ing it all the time.

MONICA: Uch. You think?

LIBBY: He *is* holding her awfully familiar.

MONICA: I *know*; he *is*. I just can't believe people do it so quickly anymore.

LIBBY: You were in the ladies' room.

MONICA: So?

LIBBY: When was the last time you saw a condom machine in a ladies' room?

MONICA: I never noticed.

LIBBY: Oh, come on.

MONICA: No, really, I never noticed. I thought people weren't having sex anymore.

LIBBY: No, people *are* having sex; you and *I* aren't having sex anymore. *(A beat) That's* an attractive couple.

MONICA: Where?

LIBBY: The Kevin Costner-looking guy in white and the woman with quite a butt.

MONICA: Oh, yeah, they are. You think they're on their honey-moon or something?

LIBBY: Maybe.

MONICA: They do look good together, don't they.

*(Libby nods. They watch the couple for a long beat.)*

How old do you think they are? Younger than us?

LIBBY: I hate to say it.

MONICA: I think so, too.

LIBBY: I like *him*.

MONICA: That's 'cause he looks so happily married.

LIBBY: That's right. Uh-oh, don't look now.

MONICA: What.

LIBBY: We're being scoped.

MONICA: You're kidding.

LIBBY: The guys with the glasses diagonally across.

MONICA: Oh my God, you're right.

LIBBY: Staring straight at us.

MONICA: Can you believe that? I thought that went out in the high school cafeteria.

LIBBY: Got our attention, didn't it.

MONICA: What should we do?

LIBBY: Does either of them interest you in any way?

MONICA: I don't know. I can't tell. They look alike.

LIBBY: I know. *(A beat)* Do we want to pursue this?

MONICA: I don't know, do we? I mean, hell, we *are* on vacation.

LIBBY: What is that supposed to mean?

MONICA: I mean, I want to *dance*! We're supposed to be enjoying ourselves.

LIBBY: Do those guys look like we'd enjoy ourselves?

*(They look at them for a moment.)*

MONICA: Good question.

LIBBY: Do they?

MONICA: Well, the one with the high forehead?

LIBBY: Yeah?

MONICA: Looks like he might have a nice smile.

LIBBY: It's not his *smile* I'm interested in, Monica. *(They giggle like schoolgirls)* Uh-oh.

MONICA: What.

LIBBY: They're coming over.

MONICA: Oh, shit.

### SCENE 4
*Outside Their Hotel Room*

*Later that night. A DO NOT DISTURB sign hangs from the door-knob. Libby is beside herself. She paces, looks at her watch, knocks at the door several times.*

LIBBY: Monica? Monica, open the door. Come on. *(A beat. Another knock)* Monica? Please don't make me use my key and walk in on you. I know you're in there. I have my key, Monica, don't make me use it. That would really be gross. *(A beat. Another knock)* Monica, open up, it's quarter to four, *please*, I want to go to bed. The deal was three. I gave you an extra forty-five minutes, *please*, Monica.

*(Monica, wrapped in a sheet, opens the door.)*

MONICA: Shhh. Steve is sleeping.
LIBBY: I don't *care* Steve is sleeping, wake him up.
MONICA: I can't just wake him up.
LIBBY: Why not? God, Monica, it's almost four o'clock in the morning—
MONICA: Shhh.
LIBBY: —and I want to go to sleep in my own bed in my own hotel room that I paid half of!
MONICA: What happened to Bruce?
LIBBY: Bruce was an asshole.
MONICA: Why?
LIBBY: Please would you just wake him up.
MONICA: What happened?
LIBBY: Nothing happened. Would you please just hand him his pants?
MONICA: Are you okay?
LIBBY: No I'm not okay. I'm tired. I want to go to sleep.

MONICA: When you didn't come at three, I figured you were staying in *their* room.

LIBBY: Why would I stay in *their* room?

MONICA: I don't know.

LIBBY: You thought I was gonna *sleep* with that asshole?

MONICA: I thought he seemed nice.

LIBBY: God, Monica.

MONICA: I thought you two looked like you really hit it off.

LIBBY: What's your definition of really hitting it off? What, 'cause I didn't throw up?

MONICA: Libby . . . *(A beat)* I'm really sorry you didn't have a nice time.

LIBBY: Will you stop taking everything so personal?! You don't have to tell me you're sorry!

MONICA: That's not what I mean. I mean I *did* have a nice time. I'm *having* a nice time. Steve is very nice. *(Pause)* Really, Libby, when you didn't come to the room at three, Steve and I, we just assumed.

LIBBY: What did you and Steve assume.

MONICA: *You* know. That you and Bruce. That you were having as nice a time as we were having.

*(A beat.)*

LIBBY: Bruce left around 12:30.

MONICA: You're kidding, he left you in the bar?

LIBBY: Uh-huh.

MONICA: Why?

LIBBY: I didn't want to sleep with him. I told him if he thought he was gonna get me in bed that he might as well give up now and go to sleep or try to pick somebody else up.

MONICA: And?

LIBBY: And he thanked me for my honesty and said good night.

MONICA: Uch, you're kidding me.

LIBBY: No.

MONICA: So you've been sitting in the bar all this time?

LIBBY: I had to come up. They were washing the floor.

MONICA: Oh God, I'm sorry. I mean, *you* know. *(A beat)* Hey, tomorrow Steve and I are gonna go snorkeling. You want to come?

*(A beat.)*

LIBBY: No, thanks.

MONICA: You sure?

LIBBY: Positive.

MONICA: 'Cause I'm sure he wouldn't mind.

LIBBY: Gee, that's very thoughtful of you.

*(A beat.)*

MONICA: You mean it?

LIBBY: What do *you* think? *(Long pause) Look* at you.

MONICA: What.

LIBBY: With your sheet and everything. You look like Julia Roberts or something.

MONICA: Yeah?

LIBBY: So, are you gonna wake him up or what?

MONICA: I guess.

*(Pause. She stays put.)*

LIBBY: Well?

*(Pause. Monica reluctantly turns to reenter the room.)*

Monica?

MONICA: Yeah?

LIBBY: Something I didn't tell you about me and Mike in the Xerox room.

*(A beat.)*

MONICA: Yeah? . . .

*(Pause.)*

LIBBY: He kissed me. With his tongue and everything.

*(Long pause. Monica returns to the room, closing the door behind her.)*

### SCENE 5
*On a Plane*

*Libby is wearing headphones and looking out the window. Monica is applying polish to her nails.*

AIRPLANE PILOT'S VOICE: Ladies and gentlemen, we're still circling over the New York area awaiting clearance to land. We're next in line, though, so we should be on the ground in, oh I'd say, eight to ten minutes. Sorry for the inconvenience, folks. At this time, on behalf of the flight crew and myself, I'd like to thank you for flying United, and wish you a happy and a healthy New Year. We'd also like to wish you good luck in the New York City area, or whatever your final destination might be.

*(The women sit in silence.)*

# L.A.

*L.A.* was commissioned and first presented by New Writers at the Westside in New York City, on November 18, 1985. It was directed by Olympia Dukakis. Man A was played by John Heard and Woman B was played by Deborah Hedwall.

*A bar in Los Angeles. A man (A) and a woman (B), both in their thirties. She chain smokes. He's looking at a photo in his wallet when she begins talking to him. He sounds vaguely southern.*

B: Texas?

A: No.

B: Not Texas? *(A shakes his head)* Arkansas?

A: *Ark*ansas?

B *(Laughing)*: No?

A: No.

B: Say a little more.

A: "A little more."

B: No, say more words, let me hear you talk.

A: I don't know what to *say* . . .

*(A beat.)*

B: Tennessee?

*(A beat. A puts his wallet in his pocket.)*

A: New Jersey.

B: What?!

A: New Jersey, I'm from New Jersey.

B: New *Jer*sey?!

A: Trenton, New Jersey.

B: You are *kid*ding me.

A: I was *born* in Yonkers.

B: You were born in *Yonk*ers?!

161

A: Uh-huh. My mother was at my grandmother's. Her water, *you* know, that's where it broke.

B: Isn't that wild? *(A shrugs)* I mean New Jersey. Who would ever've thought that you were from New Jersey?

A: This is how I talk.

B: You don't put it on?

A: Un-uh.

B: Not even a little?

A: I swear. *(Shrugs)*

*(Pause.)*

B: Now me.

A: What.

B: Guess where I'm from. Guess.

A: Florida?

B: How'd you know? *(A shrugs)* That is amazing.

A: I got a good ear—

B: This is freaky.

A: —for dialects.

B: I am freaking. What else do you know about me? *(A shrugs)* Hmm?

*(A beat.)*

A: You smoke too much.

B: I'm sorry.

A: That's all right.

B *(Putting out her cigarette)*: No, I'm really sorry. I should've asked.

A *(Overlapping "I should've")*: Really, it's no problem. I was just saying . . . an observation, that's all . . .

B *(Overlapping "that's all")*: You're right, though. You're right. I *do* smoke too much.

A *(Overlapping "I do")*: No, please. Don't put it out on account of me. Smoke. I was just saying, that's all. I was just commenting.

B: You sure?

A: I'm sure.

B: It's not disgusting?

A: No.

B: You sure? *(A nods)* I just want you to know I'm generally more polite than this. I mean, I *do* ask.

A: You were smoking already. Don't apologize.

B: The minute you mind you'll tell me?

A: Yeah.

B: Promise?

A: Promise.

*(B lights up a new cigarette. Pause.)*

Nicholson's from New Jersey, too, you know.

B: Yeah? Oh, yeah.

A: And he doesn't sound it either.

B: No, that's true.

A: Maybe it's something in the water makes us talk like this.

B *(Overlapping "makes us")*: You do not sound like you come from New Jersey, I'll tell you that.

A: I worked with him.

B: Who?

A: Jack. Nicholson. I did a picture with him.

B: Oh, yeah?

A: *Goin' South.*

B: Don't know it.

A: The one he directed.

B: Uh-huh. Didn't see it.

A *(Dropping the subject)*: Well, anyway . . .

*(Pause.)*

B: So, you acted with him? That must've been exciting.

A: The best.

B: I bet.

A: Nicholson, Belushi.

B: *Belushi*—Belushi?

A: John Belushi, yeah.

B: You knew John Belushi?

A: He was in it, too.

B: Wow. I didn't realize that. What's the name of it again?

A: *Goin' South*. Mary Steenburgen? It was her first picture.

B: Wow. I'll have to rent it.

A: Mary, Danny DeVito . . .

B: Wow. All these people.

A: Great people.

B: And you.

A: And me. *(Pause)* It was a gas.

B: I bet.

A: Boy did we tear up New Mexico.

B: Oh, yeah?

A: Place 'll never be the same. Every night, every day, partying all the time. Did a lot of drugs. A *lot* of drugs.

B: You do a lot of drugs?

A: Did.

B: Not anymore?

A: Nah. A drink, a couple of drinks . . .

B: You don't do heavy stuff do you?

A: Then I did. What, it was a six-week shoot? It was like six weeks in Disneyland. Stoned all the time. Great stuff. The stuff that was available . . . great stuff.

B: But you're not into it anymore?

A: Nah. I don't *need* it. You know? Picture was over, I stopped. Just like that. It was good while it lasted. I never did a picture before. I mean, I was straight out of New York City . . . a showcase here and there, tending bar, you know, the classic actor story, right?

B: Perfect.

A: I mean, I never starved, I paid my rent. Maybe I ate Shredded Wheat for supper every night, but I never starved. A lot

of people, friends of mine?, a lot of people had it worse.
I worked. Always doing something. Happy as a clam.

B: Uh-huh.

A: Didn't *have* anything, didn't *need* anything. I could've gone
on like that for years and it would've been okay with me.
Honestly.

B: Uh-huh.

A: Do I seem like an honest guy to you?

B: Honest?

A: Do I?

B: Yeah, I guess.

A *(Lost in thought for a beat, then back on track)*: So what was
I saying?

B: New York. The big break.

A: Right. See, I was doing the 982nd showcase of *Hatful of
Rain*, and this casting agent's assistant's assistant's lover
or something happened to see it. Next thing I knew, got
sent up for the Nicholson picture.

B: Wow. I guess these things *do* happen.

A: Met with Jack once, twice, a third time. Hit it off like we
were old buddies I'm telling you, he's like that.

B: He *seems* like that.

A: Got the picture, went to New Mexico. When it was done
everybody said why don't I give L.A. a shot.

B: Me, too, that's why *I'm* here: giving it a shot.

A: So I hung out, goofing off mostly. Audition here and there.
One day had a callback at Paramount?

B: Yeah . . . ?

A: You're gonna like this.

B: I will?

A: Very Hollywood.

B: What.

A: There she was.

B: Who?

A: The most beautiful girl in the world.

B: Oh.

A: Holding a clipboard, checking things off.

B: Uh-huh.

A: A P.A. Like a mirage.

B: A mirage with a clipboard.

A: I mean, she was so beautiful, her hair, her face.

B: Uh-huh.

A: I know it sounds corny, she was like the girl of my dreams. Like if I created a woman, she would've looked just like Sandy. Took one look at her and I was hooked, that was it, I was gone. All I wanted was her.

B *(Looking for the waiter)*: I need a refill.

A: Went up and talked to her?, it was like I'd known her all my life.

B: I can't believe you knew I was from Florida.

A: Had her in my head so perfect all my life and there she was. Asked her out? Turned me down, she was seeing some guy. I didn't care. Sent her mail-grams, flower-grams, candy-grams, balloon-grams. Sent her postcards, little notes. I mean, when I look back on it, it was pretty romantic.

B: Sounds it. It really does.

A: She finally went out with me?

B: Yeah? . . .

A: Got married three weeks later.

B: Oh, shit. You're married?

A: No, listen. See, we got married, then I got this series, like right after.

B: I recognized you. That's how come I said hello.

A *(Overlapping "I said")*: Uh-huh. So, I was on a roll. All of a sudden I was making all this money. I mean, I went from unemployment to you know how much I was making?

B: How much?

A: Guess.

B: I don't know.

A: I'll tell you, not because I'm bragging or anything. I don't brag. I'm not a bragger.

B: No.

A: I'll tell you, only 'cause I can hardly believe it myself.

B: How *much*?

A: In two years on this series?

B: Yeah? . . .

A: And it was just a small little role really.

B: How *much*?!

A: Made close to four hundred grand.

B: What?!

A: Four hundred thousand dollars.

B: That's unbelievable.

A: Before taxes.

B: That's still unbelievable.

A: And take out for my agent.

B: Still.

A: That's gross.

B: So much money!

A: I know. It's embarrassing almost.

B: Why should you be embarrassed?

A: I don't know. That's for doing a stupid little role week after
    week. It doesn't seem right.

B: Oh, the hell with it.

A: We're talking about a nothing series. I know what it is, I don't
    kid myself. I mean, some of these people doing some of
    the worst garbage, you should hear them, it's like they're
    doing *Hamlet* or something.

B: I would love to get even a little tiny part. I don't kid myself
    either. The whole medium . . .

A: I mean my series, it's *okay*.

B: Uh-huh.

A: It's not like something I'm really really proud of.

B: Of course not. It's a living.

A: Yeah, but who needs all that money. I'm an actor.

B: Hey, I'm dying to get *any*thing. You're very lucky.

A: I *am* lucky.

B: You're very lucky.

A: I don't mean to complain.

B: I know.

A: I'm just commenting. This is the situation. There are too many rich people out here.

B: In the medium?

A: In the medium, in the field. Too much money, too many *things*. It's no good.

B: Ultimately, you mean.

A: Yeah. I mean, you should drive around Bel Air.

B: I have!

A: You should see how these people live.

B: I know!

A: I mean, I like money, sure. I love money. I want nice things.

B: So do *I*.

A: I mean we *all* want nice things.

B: *I* do.

A: The American Dream and everything.

B: The American Dream, that's *right* . . .

A: It's true.

B: Oh I know.

A: There's truth in the American Dream.

B: You're looking at another sucker who bought it.

A: I mean it's real.

B: Very real, yes. We all want things, we all aspire.

A: Yes.

B: Why do you think I came to Hollywood.

A: The same thing.

B: To seek fame and fortune.

A: We work and we want to be rewarded.

B: We feel we *deserve*.

A: That's right. We all want to live nice and give our kids whatever we can possibly give them. My little girl . . .

B: You have a little girl? I didn't know you had a little girl.

A *(Takes out wallet, shows her the photo)*: Almost two.

B: Oh, my God, she's so beautiful.

A: Next month she'll be two. That right? Yeah, the 28th.

B: She is darling.

A: Katie her name is.

B: Katie.

A: I love this kid. She cracks me up.

B: Yeah? Wait, I'm not done. *(Meaning the picture)*

A: I am so crazy about her. I got her more toys . . .

B: I bet.

A: Her room is like a toy store. And she's so small. You can't find her. See, I'm the kind of father, I see something makes me think of her, I buy it. Not just dolls and stuff. Posters, paintings. Things I think she'll appreciate when she's older. I can't help it. I'm always buying her things.

B: That's nice.

A: I don't know, I try to stop but I can't.

B: You're always *think*ing of her.

A: Yeah, but maybe enough is enough. I bought her a pony.

B: Wow.

A: I think maybe I shouldn't've. My wife's allergic, so she can't take care of it. And Katie's too small. So I had to hire someone. That adds up after a while.

B: I love horses.

A: Whoever invented credit cards . . . I mean, I see something, I whip out the plastic and I don't even think twice. I love buying presents.

B: You're a generous person.

A: I don't know, think maybe I go overboard. I know I do.

B: Not necessarily.

A: I *do*. I see something I like, I want it, I got to have it. My wife and I . . . You ever been to Beverly Hills?

B: Sure.

A: Well, I just *had* to live in Beverly Hills. Don't know why, I got this idea in my head I'm a successful TV star now and I got to live in Beverly Hills.

B: The American Dream thing.

A: That's right.

B: You *deserve* to live in Beverly Hills.

A: I guess. Well, so, I got the most beautiful house. One look, I knew I had to have it. A real house. My first real house. Four bedrooms, pool, garden. I love that house. But not only do you buy the house, but you got to pay for the gardener, and the housekeeper, and the babysitter, and the insurance, and then you need a couple of cars . . . I got her this custom pink Mercedes for our anniversary. Had a fit but she loves it. I mean, I kind of went on this spree. Thought, What the hell, it's only money. I mean I went nuts. I love gadgets. VCRs, microwaves, big-screen TVs, state-of-the-art stereo, state-of-the-art burglar alarm. It was fun in the beginning. We used to joke about it. I was like a guy at the craps table. Or a coke fiend or something. I mean, some people blow their dough on dope. Not me, that doesn't interest me. If I want to get stoned, I got friends I can visit. You know what I mean?

B: Uh-huh.

A: I got friends for that. That's not my idea of what I want out of life. I like things that *last*. Not something that lasts as long as a high. I mean cameras, a synthesizer, because I want to get back into music.

B: You're into music? I sing!

A: Truth is, this computer I bought, it's still in the *box*. Got it almost a year ago. See, I went too far and I know it. Went completely overboard. My credit stopped. One day, just like that, like the well was dry.

B: Hmm.

A: My wife threw me out.

B: Oh no.

A: Oh, this is a while ago. Really woke me up, I tell you. A real slap in the face. I mean when something like that happens you stop and say to yourself, Whoa!, hey, man, you're going over the deep end. Really opened my eyes.

B: Uh-huh.

A: I told her, "Honey, you really opened my eyes. I'll change. I understand my problem now."

170

B: Uh-huh.

A: Divorced me anyhow.

B: Oh . . .

A: You know how much a divorce costs?

B: I can imagine.

A: I'm not even gonna tell you 'cause it would make you sick and I don't want you losing all that good alcohol. A lot of money. A *lot* of money. Lawyers and lawyers and more lawyers. You ever deal with a lawyer?

B: Legally? No.

A: Assholes. One asshole's bigger than the one before. Don't ever need a lawyer. What a system. Designed to destroy people.

B: What.

A: How divorce works. They want to destroy me. Did I tell you my series got canceled today?

B: Oh, no, you didn't.

A: I'm not worried. I always got *some*thing. What did I need all that money for anyway? All I've got now is this little studio. A bed, a TV.

B: Back to basics, right?

A: Yeah. Took it so I could be near my daughter. I see her every day. My wife's cool about that, thank God. She knows I'm not gonna run away with her or anything. Though, I tell you, I've thought about it. I *have* thought about it.

B: I don't know about that. That gives me the creeps.

A: I'm an honest guy . . . I don't know, sometimes I think if I really want something . . . She's crazy about me, my little girl. *(Pause)* I tell ya, when I was knocking around New York . . .

B: Uh-huh.

A: Working here and there . . .

B: Yeah? . . .

A: I had this secret fantasy.

B: Tell me yours and I'll tell you mine.

A: I had this fantasy that one day I was gonna make it, not big, big enough, *you* know, a steady income coming in . . .

B: Uh-huh.

A: And I'd treat my friends who weren't working to a good dinner every now and then, and help 'em get work, and fall in love and get married for life, for *life,* and have a couple of kids, and give those kids everything I could give them, and live in style, not showy, but in style, and that was all I wanted. That was my secret fantasy. That's not a bad fantasy, right?

*(B shakes her head; pauses. A looks at the photo in his wallet, then puts it away. Pause.)*

So what's yours?

*(As she opens her mouth to speak:*
 *Blackout.)*

# PITCHING TO
# THE STAR

*Pitching to the Star* was first presented at the West Bank Cafe Downstairs Theatre Bar (Lewis Black and Rand Foerster, Artistic Directors) in New York City, on March 20, 1990. It was directed by Rand Foerster. The cast was as follows:

| | |
|---|---|
| DICK | Lewis Black |
| PETER | Robert Sean Leonard |
| LAURI | Mary Kane |
| DENA | Kathryn Rossetter |
| VOICES OF JENNIFER AND TYNE | Lynn Chausow |

### CHARACTERS

PETER ROSENTHAL, the writer, thirty-two
DICK FELDMAN, the producer, forties
DENA STRAWBRIDGE, the star, forties
LAURI RICHARDS, the D-Girl, twenty-eight
VOICE OF JENNIFER, Dick's secretary, thirties
VOICE OF TYNE, Dick's daughter, ten

### SETTING

The present.

The office of Dick Feldman at his home in Sherman Oaks, California.

*Dick Feldman's home office. The furnishings are mostly white.
Cans of Diet Coke litter the Santa Fe–style coffee table. A voice-
activated intercom/speaker is prominently placed on the rear wall.*

DICK: It's a courtesy thing.

PETER: Uh-huh.

DICK: No big deal. What, you're scared?

PETER: No.

DICK: You're *nervous*? *(To Lauri)* Look at him. *(Lauri laughs; to
Peter)* Dena *Straw*bridge, you're *nervous*?

PETER: No, I just didn't expect . . .

DICK: She's the *star*. So *what*? Big fucking deal. People *know*
her? She's well known? So?

PETER: I didn't think (today) I'd . . .

DICK: People know her *face*? So? She's a has-been. A druggie.
Her tits sag. Boy, this celebrity shit really impresses you,
doesn't it.

PETER *(A little p.o.'ed)*: No, it's just—

DICK: You're *really* new in town, aren't you—

PETER: I didn't think I'd have to *pitch* . . .

DICK: I'm *teasing* you. Hey. We want to *include* her a little bit,
that's all. Make her feel, *you* know, like a star, important.
So you pitch the pilot to her. Nothing to it. She likes the
pitch?, she doesn't like it?—same difference. You don't
have to sell *her*, you sold *us*. Get it?

PETER: Uh-huh.

DICK: You're *ours*, not *hers*. Remember that. You don't have to
*deal* with her, let *me* deal with her. You just be nice. Be
pleasant. Be cute. You *are* cute. She'll like you. Just be
cute, you'll see. Be yourself. She'll love you. It's not what

you *say* (you understand?), it's not what you *pitch*. Let her think we care what she thinks. (That's what today is about.) She says something? Go: "Uh-*huh*, let me think about that." She'll love you for life. Don't write it *down* even, just: "Uh-*huh*." Like: "What an interesting idea. Gee, I must give that some thought, Dena, thank you." Guarantee she won't remember what she said thirty seconds later but you made a friend for life. You were pleasant. You didn't show an attitude. You don't *want* to be her friend. Remember that. I'm talking purposes of the show solely. She's the star. You don't fuck with a star, so to speak. She, in her mind, is apart from the rest of the world. She's a star. Stars don't know *how* to be a friend. They don't *have* friends. They're suspicious of everyone. They don't *like* people. They're ambivalent about their success. They don't know what they did to *deserve* it, which makes them very suspicious of people. With good reason when you think about it: people *want* things from stars. So, consequently, as a result, they're suspicious, lonely, deeply fucked-up people. Remember: you don't *want* to be her friend. You don't need *her*. She needs *you*. *Fuck* her.

   *(Calls)* Jennifer? Jen?

JENNIFER'S VOICE *(Over intercom)*: Yes, Dick?

DICK: What time is it?

JENNIFER'S VOICE: 12:20, Dick.

DICK: *What* time?

JENNIFER'S VOICE: Twenty after twelve.

   *(Lauri shows Dick her watch.)*

DICK: She's late. *Star* shit. Already it's starting. I'm telling you, she pulls that shit with *me* . . .

PETER: So she knows about the style of the show? She knows how we want to shoot it?

DICK: Bubbie, what did I just finish saying? She doesn't know shit.

LAURI: I think what Peter's asking—

DICK: It's not like we have to con*sult* with her. We're not looking for her ap*prov*al.

PETER: I mean, she knows we're talking about a one-camera film show?

DICK: We'll get you as many cameras as you want.

PETER: I only want one.

DICK: So we'll get you one. Jesus Christ. What are you so worried about? *(To Lauri)* You ever see such a worrier?

*(Lauri laughs.)*

PETER: I'm not worried. I just want to make sure—

DICK: What, what's the problem here?

PETER: Nothing. I just want to make sure . . . Remember the very first conversation we had? I told you I wasn't interested in writing a three-camera sitcom? I'm only interested in writing a half-hour film.

LAURI: Yes, Peter feels very strongly about this, Dick.

DICK: Huh?

LAURI: Peter feels—

DICK *(To Peter)*: What are you suggesting?

PETER: I'm not suggesting anything. I just want your assurance that—

DICK: And you have it. Period. The end. I don't understand the problem here.

PETER: Dick, there's no problem. Don't misconstrue my concern.

DICK: Nobody's misconstruing anybody.

LAURI: I think what Peter is saying—

PETER: What if—just listen to me a second, indulge me, okay?—What if we pitch the show to Dena Strawbridge and she loves it, and then we say, "By the way, this is a film show," and she says, "Oh, sorry, I don't want to do a film show." What do we do?

DICK: We dump her.

PETER: Really?

DICK: She doesn't want to do it our way? Absolutely. We dump her. "Sorry, Dena," whatever. "Ah, that's too bad, we want to go for something else." That's all there is to it.

PETER: Yeah?

DICK: You worried about getting this on the air? Write it good, bubbie, it'll get on the air, Dena Strawbridge or no Dena Strawbridge. There are hundreds of has-been Dena Strawbridges out there. We can always find a new star. This is Los Angeles.

PETER: Okay.

DICK: Hundreds. Are you fucking kidding me? Look through the Players' Guide. People you thought died horribly long ago are in there, waiting for a shot like this, are you kidding?

PETER: Okay. Good.

DICK: All right? You feel better now?

PETER: Yeah.

DICK: Good. Thank God. *(To Lauri)* New York playwrights, I'm telling *you* . . . *(She laughs)*
      *(Claps his hands together; to Peter)* All right, boychick, let's hear it.

PETER: You mean *now?*

DICK: Yeah, run it by me.

PETER: Oh, okay.

DICK: What, you don't wanna?

PETER: No, I didn't know we were gonna . . .

DICK: We're going in to the network tomorrow, bubbie, we're not gonna walk in *cold.* You didn't think we were just gonna walk in . . .

PETER: No. I don't know . . . *(Making light of it)* I just got here from the *airport*, Dick. I mean, I haven't even had a chance to take a *shower.*

DICK *(Kibitzing, sort of)*: What, you're gonna be *sensitive?*

PETER: No, I'm kidding . . .

DICK: You can't pitch if you smell? Huh? You're worried you smell?

PETER: I'm *kidding* . . .

DICK: We're *friends* here. *(To Lauri)* Right?

LAURI: Absolutely.

DICK: We're *friends*. We don't *care* you smell. I'm *teasing* you. *(To Lauri)* Look at him, look how sensitive . . .

PETER: Who's sensi—okay. So . . . You mind if I refer to my notes?

DICK: Go 'head.

PETER *(Takes out notes)*: I promise tomorrow I'll be more "up." I'll be *rested*, I'll be *bathed* . . .

DICK *(To Lauri)*: Boy, this guy is a real (whatayacallit?) a cleanliness freak or something. *(Lauri laughs)* A shower fetishist.

PETER: I'm kidding . . .

DICK: I *know* you're kidding, bubbie, I *know*. *I'm* kidding. *(To Lauri)* He's stalling. Look at how he's stalling.

PETER *(Launching into the pitch)*: Okay. *Working Mom*.

DICK: What is this, a *book* report? *(To Lauri, who laughs)* He's doing a book report. *(To Peter) Only kidding.* Go 'head. Great so far, I love it. I love that title. *(To Lauri)* Don't *you*?

LAURI: Great title.

DICK *(To Peter)*: Go 'head. Sorry. No more interruptions.

PETER: Okay. So—

DICK *(Calls)*: Jen?

JENNIFER'S VOICE: Yes, Dick?

DICK *(Calls)*: Hold all calls.

JENNIFER'S VOICE: I am, Dick.

DICK *(To Peter)*: All yours, pal.

PETER: Okay, here we go. *(Clears throat)* What we hope to do with *Working Mom*, what we hope to *accomplish*, is to explore, in very real terms, what it means to be a single, working-class working mother today.

*(Dick takes the notes out of Peter's hands and looks them over.)*

DICK: What *is* this?

PETER: These are the notes I sent you.

DICK: What notes?

PETER: I FedExed them to you two weeks ago. I don't have a fax, remember? You wanted them as quickly as possible.

DICK: How come *I* never saw these notes?

LAURI: I gave them to you, Dick. Remember?

DICK: All I can say is I never saw these notes.

LAURI: I *gave* them to you.

DICK: And I'm telling you I never saw them.

LAURI: They were right on your desk. I *put* them on your desk.

DICK: And I never *saw* them, okay? I never *saw* them. *(Hands them back to Peter)* You should've gotten feedback on this.

PETER: When I didn't hear from you, I assumed they were okay.

DICK: Never assume. I'm saying I'm sorry. The error occurred in this office.

LAURI: I put them on your desk, Dick.

DICK *(To Peter)*: Go on.

PETER: Um . . . to explore, in very real terms—

DICK: I'm not sure about this "explore" shit . . .

PETER: No?

DICK: Sounds so . . . surgical. This is *comedy*, man.

PETER: I know. I'm just trying to . . .

DICK: You do this at the network (I'll be perfectly honest with you) . . . You do this at the network tomorrow, you might as well hand out pillows and blankies and tuck everybody in.

PETER: I said I'll have more energy tomorrow.

DICK: Fuck energy. Excuse me. I'm not talking energy or no energy. *The pitch has got to entertain.* Believe me. I've been doing this a lot longer than you have.

PETER: I know . . .

DICK: If you don't grab them from the word go . . .

LAURI: It's true.

DICK *(To Lauri)*: Am I right?

LAURI: Absolutely. It has to—

DICK: This is key: *you have to make it sound like fun.* These guys don't know. You think they know shit? You have to show them *the potential for fun.* They need to know it's okay to enjoy themselves. You need to smile.

PETER: Smile?

DICK: Yeah. You look like you're sitting shiva.

PETER: I do? I'm sorry.

DICK: Hey. That's okay. That's what I'm here for. That's what today is about. These are things to keep in mind. Go on.

PETER *(Continuing)*: Dena Flanders was a junior at Atlantic City High when she got pregnant for the first time. Her boyfriend, Paulie Vanzetti, married her and, even though they had two more kids, Paulie never could stop gambling and chasing cocktail waitresses. Dena's finally had it. She moves herself and her kids into her mother's house. All she wants is to get her life back on track. So, with the help of her tart-tongued mother (Olympia Dukakis), Dena takes night classes to finish her high school degree. In the pilot, she gets a job as a paralegal in the storefront office of a crusty old leftie attorney named Al Sapirstein (Jerry Stiller).

DICK: Wait a second.

PETER: Yeah?

DICK: Pete. Hold it. *(Pause)* You know that *play* of yours?

PETER: Which one?

DICK: The one I flipped over. The Jewish guy?

PETER: *Shabbos Goy?*

DICK: *Shabbos Boy*, that's right.

PETER: *Goy.*

LAURI: *Goy*, Dick.

DICK: Funny play. You had some scenes in there . . .

PETER: Thank you.

DICK: You're a funny guy.

PETER: Thanks.

DICK *(To Lauri)*: Isn't he a funny guy?

LAURI: Oh God, are you kidding?

DICK: Very funny guy. And funny is money. *(To Lauri)* No?

LAURI: Definitely.

DICK *(To Peter)*: Let me tell *you*: funny is money, my friend, and you are funny.

PETER: Well, thanks.

DICK: When I discovered that script of yours . . . Howling! I was howling!

PETER: Really?

DICK: Uh! Funny funny stuff.

PETER: Thanks.

DICK: *Now*: you know how you wrote in your play?

PETER: Yeah? . . . What.

DICK: You know how *funny* you wrote?

PETER: Yeah? . . .

DICK: Do that here.

PETER: What.

DICK: Do that *here*. Be *funny*. Write funny. This isn't funny.

PETER: It may not *sound* funny . . .

DICK: No. This is not funny.

PETER: When I *write* it . . .

DICK *(To Lauri)*: You think this is funny?

LAURI: Well I understand what he's—

DICK: No. It's not. Pete. Listen to me. You don't understand. Make this funny. What you've got *here* (believe me, I know what I'm talking about), it isn't funny. Plain and simple. No matter how you cut it. When you write it (believe me), it's gonna suck. Just think of your play. I read it. I know what you can do. Do what you did there.

TYNE'S VOICE *(Over intercom)*: Daddy?

DICK: You can do it, Pete. *(Calls)* Yes, baby.

TYNE'S VOICE: Daddy, Consuelo says I can't have Mrs. Fields. She says it's for supper.

DICK: It *is* for supper, Tyney. For coffee after. *(A beat)* Tyne? *(He listens, Tyne's gone; he takes off shoes, lays down on sofa)* So, *good* so far. Let's hear the pilot. Pitch me the pilot.

PETER: Okay. So. The opening. I thought it would be fun if we opened with sort of a parody of that great sweeping pan of the Statue of Liberty that opens *Working Girl?* Remember the opening of *Working Girl?*

LAURI: Uh-huh.

PETER: Well, I thought what we could do for *Working MOM* is the camera swoops really dramatically around the statue and then, instead of heading over to the Manhattan skyline, it ends up in New Jersey.

LAURI: Oooh. Nice. Isn't that nice, Dick?

PETER: *You* know, kind of working-class, industrial New Jersey. Refineries, highways, smog sunset. So there's a kind of irony there, from the word go, that tells us that this isn't gonna be another glossy single-working-mother kind of show. The irony is you think—

DICK: Wait wait wait. "Irony"? *(To Lauri)* He's an intellectual. *(She laughs)* Intellectuals (what can I tell you?) they love "irony." *(She laughs even more)* I don't give a *shit* "irony."

PETER: I was just—

DICK: Excuse me. You pushed a button. I'm very emotional about this. You pushed a—there it goes! You will learn this about me, Peter. Ask anybody who's worked with me. They will tell you the same: I do not bullshit. *(To Lauri; meaning "True?")* Huh?

LAURI: It's true.

DICK *(To Peter)*: Hey, I don't mean to blow you away.

PETER: No, I'm all right . . .

DICK *(To Lauri)*: He's looking at me like God knows . . . *(To Peter)* I'm your *friend* for telling you this. I know you're just off the plane so to speak. You're new in this town. Save your "irony" for the *stage.* Okay? (I'm about to save you a lot of grief.) Save it for the *theatre.* That's all I have to say on the subject. Period, end quote. I don't bullshit people I like, I have *respect* for. *(To Lauri)* Am I right?

LAURI: Oh, absolutely.

DICK: I don't have time for irony. Give me a story. Tell me a good story, I'm happy. That's all I ask: give me a good story. Whatever happened to stories? Hmm? Remember stories? Bubbeleh, this is what I'm telling you. We gotta clear your brain of that shit. We gotta vacuum it out. Simple stories, Peter. Where a cow is a cow for a change. Boy meets girl. Yeah. No symbols. No irony. One thing doesn't mean another. Who wants to sit there (no really now), who wants to have to *sit* there and *work* and figure it out? "Oh, I get it: the so-and-so really means the *Holocaust*." "Child abuse." Fill in the blank. Fuck it. Life is too short for irony. Please. Tell me the fucking story. *This* happens, then *this* happens, then *this* happens, so-on and so-forth. People after a hard day, they do not want to have to put on their thinking caps. *(Getting up, unzipping his fly)* These are important lessons in this town, pal . . . I swear one day you're gonna thank me. *(To Lauri)* Look at him, he hates me. *(Lauri laughs)* Fucking Diet Cokes . . .

*(While reaching into his fly, Dick exits to the bathroom. A beat.)*

LAURI: You know Dick's never done TV before.
PETER: What do you mean?
LAURI: He's done *movies*.
PETER: Oh, yeah, I know.
LAURI: He had that one Tom Cruise thing, he got this deal as a result.
PETER: Uh-huh.
LAURI: Sure, he was kicking around for years (who hasn't).
PETER: Uh-huh.
LAURI: But the truth is . . . when it comes to television . . . ?
PETER: Yeah? . . .
LAURI: He doesn't know the first thing.
PETER: Oh, really.

LAURI: Not a thing. It's embarrassing. I *work* for this guy. I *work* for him. We go into these meetings at the network?

PETER: Yeah? . . .

LAURI: And it's like *unbelievable.*

PETER: Huh. *(Meaning "How do you like that?")*

LAURI: The guy. Doesn't. Know. The business. Television, I mean. Okay, so he had a hit movie. A lot of people have hit movies, doesn't make them experts in *television.* What does *he* know about *television?* He thinks he knows how to put together a *series?* It's a joke. I'm saving his ass all over town. I'm covering for him. I have to call the network after we meet with them?

PETER: Yeah? . . .

LAURI: To like patch-up for all the schmucky things he said? It's a joke. I was instrumental in *Charles in Charge—before* it went into syndication! I was *there*, learning, paying my dues, seeing how it's done. What does *Dick* know? Do you think he knows good material when he sees it? I have to *tell* him what's good. I have to *find* what's good (but that's not enough). *I have to get him to read it.* A writer doesn't *exist* out here until he's read. They don't know New York theatre. I really had to fight for you, you know.

PETER: Oh, yeah? How do you mean?

LAURI: *I'm* the one who kept on pushing your play on him.

PETER: Well, thank you.

LAURI: These people don't read. They do *not* read. I was in Theatre, you know.

PETER: Oh, yeah? Where'd you go to school?

LAURI: B.U.?

PETER: Uh-huh.

LAURI: I always felt that we could really break ground with *Working Mom,* we could really do some important television—*if* we found the right writer for the pilot. Someone who's fresh and doesn't know all the sitcom tricks. We wanted you because you *don't* know the formula. You *don't* know the tricks. We wanted *grit* and humor *and* ethnicity, *authenticity*. You've got it all.

PETER: Thanks.

LAURI: You *do.* "Peter Rosenthal is who we want for *Working Mom*," I said. No, "Peter Rosenthal is who we *need*. If we don't get Peter Rosenthal—and he's very hot right now—" (This is what I told him.) "—If we don't *nab* him (and if we don't, we're idiots), if we don't fly him out here *right away*, then I ask you: my God, what are we all doing here?" *(Grasps his wrist; confidentially)* Peter?

PETER: Yes, Lauri?

LAURI: Feel free to call me any time. You have my home number?

PETER: Yeah, I think you . . .

LAURI: Any time.

PETER: You wrote it on your card.

LAURI: You're gonna need someone to talk to out here.

PETER: I appreciate that, Lauri, but I have friends . . .

LAURI: No, I mean, these things can get pretty intense. Development, I mean. It can get dirty. You can get hurt if you don't watch out.

PETER: Thanks, Lauri.

LAURI: Hey, I feel responsible. I'm the one who got you out here. We have to protect writers like you. Do you know how *rare* it is to find a writer like you? I *cherish* writers. Writers are all we have. Really, when you think about it. Promise you'll call me.

PETER: I promise.

LAURI: Peter, you have *such* a unique comic *voice*, I can't tell you.

PETER: Thank you.

LAURI: No, thank *you*. You have no idea how many scripts I read. And it's all shit. Then to discover someone like you?! It's like: "Oh, yeah, right, *this* is why I want to produce. *This* is why I came out here."

*(The toilet flushes. Dick returns.)*

DICK: What's this?

LAURI: Nothing. I was just telling Peter what a unique voice we think he has.

DICK: Oh, yeah. Really unique. So, where are we?

JENNIFER'S VOICE: Dena's here, Dick.

DICK: In the house or on her way?

JENNIFER'S VOICE: *Here.*

DICK: Shit.

LAURI *(To Peter)*: Don't worry.

*(Dena Strawbridge, brittle, nervous, early forties, enters.)*

DENA: Hi. Sorry. I was at Pritikin.

DICK: Hey. Dena. There's my girl. *(He hugs her)* Oh, man, so good to see you.

DENA: Good to see you, too.

DICK: You're looking sensational.

DENA: Yeah? Oh . . .

DICK *(To Lauri)*: Doesn't she look—?

LAURI: Mmm, yes!

DENA: Thank you. Do I know you?

DICK: My development exec, Lauri Richards?

DENA: Oh, hi.

LAURI: Hello. Really nice to meet you finally.

DENA: Thank you.

DICK: And, Dena? Remember that *terrific* young writer we told you about? From New York?

DENA: Yes!

DICK: This is Peter Rosenthal. From New York.

PETER: Hi. Nice to meet you.

DENA: Thank you. Wow. Really really nice to meet you, too . . .

DICK: So! We were just pitching, the three of us.

DENA: Oh, yeah?

DICK: Sounds great.

DENA: Yeah?

DICK: Uh! You're gonna love it.

DENA: Oooh! I can't wait. *(Grasping Dick's hand) God,* am I glad we're working together . . . *(He hugs her again)*

DICK: Me, too. Didn't I tell you we *would* one day?

DENA: I am so so excited about this project. You mind if I eat? *(She takes out her lunch)*

DICK: No. Eat. What is that?

DENA: Oh, I'm on macro. It's great. You ever do it?

DICK: No.

DENA: Oh, it's great. I'm keeping my weight down, I'm more regular than I've ever been in my entire life . . . It's great. Really. You should try it. I'll give you my nutritionist's number. He's fabulous. Oh! I have regards for you!

DICK: Oh, yeah? From who?

DENA: Joel Kaplan?

DICK: Joel Kaplan, no shit! How do you know Joel?

DENA: He produced my miniseries.

DICK: No kidding, is that so?

DENA: Yeah, and he's looking really good. Have you seen him lately?

DICK: He's had a hell of a time.

DENA: I know, but he's looking great. I just ran into him at Pritikin. He lost something like fifty pounds.

DICK: No kidding. Good for him. *(To Peter and Lauri)* This guy was a fat fucking pig.

DENA: He's seeing Leonard, too. My nutritionist. Remind me to give you his number, you will love him.

DICK: Gee, I really should give Joel a call . . . Where *is* he now?

DENA: Warners.

DICK: I thought he was at Universal.

DENA: That deal ran out. He got an even better deal at Warners. An *incredible* deal. And he looks really really great.

DICK *(Calls)*: Jennifer?

JENNIFER'S VOICE: Yes, Dick?

DICK *(Calls)*: Put Joel Kaplan on my call list? *(To Dena)* Warners?

DENA: Uh-huh.

DICK *(Calls)*: He's at Warners. *(To Dena)* Is he clean now, Joel?

DENA: Oh, yeah. You should see him.

DICK: I heard he had his nose redone.

DENA: Oh, yeah, he was in big big trouble. He was killing himself.

DICK: I didn't know it got so bad.

DENA: The man was killing himself.

DICK: Jeez . . . *(To Peter)* Joel Kaplan? You know him?

PETER: No.

DICK: Biggest asshole alive.

DENA: Well . . . he did a great job on my miniseries.

DICK: Good.

DENA: A super super job. Considering what he was going through.

DICK: I'm glad he came through for you, Dena. I'm truly glad to hear that.

DENA: Absolutely terrific.

DICK: I'm an asshole: tell me the name again?

DENA: *The Deadly Weekend of Marilyn Monroe?*

DICK: Oh, of course!

LAURI: Oh, yes!

DICK: I *am* an asshole! That was supposed to be . . .

DENA: I know.

DICK *(To Lauri)*: Did you see that?

LAURI: No, I was in the hospital for my lumpectomy.

DICK: We heard that was terrific! *(To Lauri)* Didn't we hear that was terrific?

LAURI: Oh, yes! Everybody was—

DENA: It won me my Emmy nomination so I guess it must've been pretty—

DICK: Yeah, congratulations on that!

LAURI AND PETER: Congratulations.

DENA: *Thank* you.

DICK: Did you win it?, I forget.

DENA: No, no. Katharine Hepburn got it that year. But, I tell you, I was so honored just to be *nominated* with that lady.

189

LAURI: Hmm, yeah.

DICK: Wow. Now I want to see it.

DENA: I was so frigging proud. A role like that doesn't come along very often for a woman, let's face it. I got to do everything. The Bobby Kennedy scenes? I mean, between takes Marty Sheen had to *hold* me, that's how much I was shaking . . .

LAURI: Wow.

DICK: Shit, I really want to see this . . . *(Calls)* Jen?

JENNIFER'S VOICE: Yes, Dick.

DICK: Call the agency, see if they can get us a copy—

DENA: No, you don't have to do that . . .

DICK: —of Dena's miniseries, *Deadly* . . .

DENA: . . . *Weekend of Marilyn Monroe.*

DICK: The Marilyn Monroe thing.

DENA: You really don't—

DICK: Tell them to messenger it over—

DENA: Dick, you really don't have to do that . . . *(To Lauri)* What a crazy nut. *(Lauri nods)*

DICK: *(Overlapping)*: —I want to look at it tonight.

DENA: You *don't* have to do this on my account.

DICK: I *want* to. Are you kidding? It'll be fun.

DENA: Well, good.

JENNIFER'S VOICE: Dick?

DICK *(Calls)*: Yeah, Jen.

JENNIFER'S VOICE: I've got Joel Kaplan for you.

DICK *(Calls)*: Joel Ka–? Who called who? *(To others)* Isn't this freaky?

JENNIFER'S VOICE: You told me to get him.

DICK *(Calls)*: I said put him on my *list,* Jennifer.

JENNIFER'S VOICE: Oh, I thought . . .

DICK *(Calls)*: Uh, look . . . I said on my list . . .

JENNIFER'S VOICE: Sorry, Dick . . . I've *got* him . . . *(A beat)* What do you want me to *do* with him?

DICK: Tell him I'll have to get back to him. I'm in a meeting.

JENNIFER'S VOICE: Okay. Sorry, Dick.

DICK *(Calls)*: Yeah. *(To others)* Jesus. Do you believe her? She can be such a flake sometimes. *Now*. This *guy* . . . *(Meaning Peter)* Are we lucky! This *boy* . . . *How* old are you?

PETER: Thirty-two.

DICK: Nah. You are not . . .

PETER: Yes, I am.

DICK: You look twenty-five, twenty-six.

PETER: I'm thirty-two, though, believe me.

DICK: Doesn't he look twenty-five?

DENA: Yeah, he does.

DICK: Twenty-five, twenty-seven *maybe* . . .

PETER: No, I'm thirty-two.

DICK: You could pass. Easy. Lie. Fib. Tell people you're twenty-five, they'll eat it up.

PETER: But I'm not.

DICK: Fib, I said. People out here, everybody's very impressed with how young you are. Everybody loves a prodigy. Say you're twenty-five, mark my words. —*Anyhow* . . . this *guy* . . . this *boy* . . . wrote a *play* . . . ran in New *York* . . . (Joe *Papp* produced this play).

DENA *(With interest)*: Uh-huh?

DICK: This *play* . . . *Shabbos Boy* . . . I'm telling you . . . had me peeing in my pants. *(To Lauri)* Right?

LAURI: It did.

DICK: Peeing! On the floor!

DENA: Really?

DICK: In my pants! *(To Lauri)* Tell her.

LAURI: It's true.

DENA: Oh, how great!

DICK: Funny, funny play.

PETER: Thanks, Dick.

DICK: Funny is money. I keep telling him that, he doesn't believe me.

PETER: I believe you.

DICK: He thinks I'm *lying* he can be a gold mine out here.

PETER: I believe you.

DICK: There's a scene he's got in this play, Dena . . .

DENA: Yeah?

DICK: Dena, this *scene* . . . with the mother?

PETER: The grandmother, actually.

DICK: Huh?

PETER: You mean with the grandmother? You told me . . .

DICK: The mother, the grandmother, whatever . . . Anyhow, he's yelling at her about his bris? *(To Dena)* Circumcision. You know, when they *perform* it, the people, they throw a party . . . ?

DENA: Oh, yeah, I know some people who did that . . .

DICK: Anyhow, he's yelling, "How could you do something like that to me!"

DENA: Oh, how funny.

DICK: And she *sits* there. She *sits* there, the mother, the grandmother, and she doesn't say a word!

PETER: Oh, you mean the stroke scene?

DICK: What?

PETER: The stroke scene. The grandmother's had a stroke. That's why she doesn't say anything.

DICK *(Thinks he's kidding)*: Nahhh . . .

PETER: Yes! She's had a stroke and he doesn't realize it. That's what the scene is about.

DICK: Oh, you mean the *stroke* scene! Sure! Oh, yeah, of course. Well, the point is (whatever): a riot. The *play* is a riot.

DENA: What's the name of it again?

PETER: *Shabbos Goy.*

DICK: *Shabbos Boy.*

PETER: *Shabbos Goy.*

DICK: *Goy?* I thought *Boy.*

PETER: No.

DICK: What does it mean? I mean, I don't know Jewish.

PETER: A shabbos goy is a non-Jew hired by Orthodox Jews to do little chores . . . like lighting the stove, turning on the electricity . . . Orthodox Jews aren't allowed to do certain

things on the Sabbath. Saturday. That's what "shabbos"
means: Saturday.

DENA: Oh! *I* get it.

DICK: That's a good title.

PETER: Thanks.

DICK: I mean, you should've called it that: *Shabbos Goy* not
*Boy*.

PETER: I did.

DICK: Wait . . . you did or you didn't?

LAURI: Dick? The name of the play *is Shabbos Goy*.

DICK: *Shabbos Goy* has irony—I mean, it, uh, has more *meaning*.

PETER: I agree. That's why I called it that.

DICK: The copy we read . . . I could swear it said "Boy." *(Calls)*
Jen? Jennifer?

JENNIFER'S VOICE: Yes, Dick.

DICK: Bring in a copy of Peter's play?

JENNIFER'S VOICE: *Shabbos Goy?*

DICK: Uh, never mind.

DENA: So, what's it about, your play?

PETER: It's a comedy, I guess. About assimilation.

DENA: Uh-huh. Neat. A comedy, huh? Isn't that kind of a tough
subject?

PETER: Well . . .

DENA: I mean, considering what's going on?

*(A beat.)*

PETER: What do you mean exactly?

DENA: I mean, *you* know, South Africa?

PETER: South Africa?

DENA: *You* know: what's going *on* over there with that.

*(A beat.)*

PETER: Oh. Apartheid?

DENA: *That's* it. *That's* the word . . .

PETER: No, my play's about Jews who have assimilated into a gentile society.

DENA: Wow. Oh. I getcha.

DICK: The Public Theater did it.

DENA: Hmm.

DICK: The Public Theater in New York? Joe Papp?

DENA: Oh, yeah. I know him. Wasn't he at Fox?

DICK: Joe Papp?

DENA: Yeah, I think he was. Short guy, right?

DICK: Yeah . . .

DENA: Yeah, he was at Fox. I'm positive.

DICK: Joe Papp?

DENA: Jewish guy, right?

DICK: Yeah . . .

DENA: I did meet him. At Fox.

PETER: I really don't think so.

DICK *(Over "think so")*: Yeah? Maybe. Whataya know? Yeah, I think you're right. Leave it to Dena. Anyhow . . . Let's hear this pitch . . . *(All eyes are on Peter)*

TYNE'S VOICE: Daddy, Consuelo ate Mrs. Fields.

DICK *(Calls)*: Tyne? Daddy's in a meeting, honey.

TYNE'S VOICE: Daddy, I want a cookie, too. I want *two* cookies.

DICK *(Overlapping; to others)*: Sorry, my kid.

DENA *(Overlapping)*: Perfectly all right.

DICK *(Calls)*: Tyne? Tyney, honey? You can have *one*.

TYNE'S VOICE: I want macadamia with dark chocolate *and* milk chocolate.

DENA: She's adorable *(Lauri nods)*

DICK: No, Tyney. One. Pick one.

TYNE'S VOICE: I want both. Consuelo had one or two, I'm not sure, and she wasn't supposed to have *any*.

DICK *(Calls)*: You can have one chocolate and one—

TYNE'S VOICE: What kind of chocolate? There's dark chocolate and milk chocolate.

DICK *(Overlapping; calls)*: Daddy's in a meeting, sweetheart, this isn't a good time for this.

TYNE'S VOICE: Daddy, it's not fair Consuelo should have—

DICK: Consuelo *shouldn't've* had, okay?! *(To others)* These fucking . . . *(Calls)* Take a chocolate chip and an oatmeal raisin and—

TYNE'S VOICE: I don't like oatmeal.

DICK: Oatmeal is healthier.

TYNE'S VOICE: I want one macadamia with dark chocolate . . .

DICK: Tyne . . .

TYNE'S VOICE: . . . and one milk chocolate chip.

DICK: Okay! Now leave Daddy alone! So what do you say? Tyne? What do you say, honey? Tyne? Tyney? *(A beat. To others)* Anyhow . . . *(To Peter)* Let's hear the pitch.

PETER: Okay. Um . . . *Working Mom* . . .

DICK *(To Dena)*: Don't you love that title?

DENA: Oh, yeah, I do.

LAURI: So do I.

DICK: I love it. *Working Mom*: it just *says* it.

DENA: It really does.

DICK *(To Peter)*: Go 'head.

PETER: Okay, and I see the opening . . . The opening's this sweeping pan of the Statue of Liberty? You know, the camera will sweep around it—

DICK *(Sort of discreetly)*: Skip it.

PETER: Hmm?

DICK: Skip it. Cut to the chase.

DENA: No, I'm with you.

DICK: I want you to hear the story. This stuff, it's trimming.

PETER: I just thought I'd give you a sense of the—

DICK: Don't worry about it. Tell the story. Like you did before. Just tell it.

DENA: Yeah, tell me who she is. I'm dying to know who she is.

PETER: All right. Um . . . Dena Flanders—

DENA *(Laughing)*: "Flanders"?

PETER: Yeah—was a junior at Atlantic City High when—

DENA: Atlantic City? Where is that again?

PETER: New Jersey.

DENA: Oh, right.

PETER: So, when she was a junior in high school—

DENA: Excuse me. Can I say something?

DICK: Sure. Go 'head. Feel free. That's what you're here for. Jump right in whenever you like.

DENA: Thanks. I was just wondering . . .

DICK: I got some Evian for you. Want some?

DENA: No, thanks. Now: why does she have to be from New Jersey?

PETER: Well . . .

DENA: I mean, like, take *me* for instance.

PETER: Uh-huh.

DENA: I'm from Wisconsin.

PETER: Yeah . . .

DENA: I mean, couldn't she be from Wisconsin?


*(A beat.)*


LAURI: Huh. Interesting.

PETER: But this *char*acter is *from* New Jersey. Where she's from has a lot to do with who she is.

DICK: I think Peter would have to think about that, wouldn't you, Peter?

PETER: Umm . . . Yeah. I'd have to think about that a lot.

DENA: You see, let me just say something—do you mind?

PETER: Not at all.

DENA: The thing about Wisconsin . . . I'm *from* Wisconsin, okay? I grew up there. I *know* it. I *lived* it. I know the *people.* I know what Wisconsin *smells* like. *(She inhales)*

PETER: Well, gee, that's interesting, I'll have to—

DENA: There's something about really really knowing a place . . . You know what I mean? You don't have to act. I mean from an acting standpoint. You do not have to *act,* it's there, it's in your skin, it's in your soul, it's *just there.*

DICK *(Taking to the idea)*: Uh-huh, uh-huh. I don't hate that.

PETER: But the story revolves around—

DICK: I don't hate that at all. I like it, in fact.

PETER: Wait, but the story . . .

DICK: The story you can always fix. I do not hate this, there's something to it.

DENA *(To Dick)*: You know what I mean?

DICK: I do. I absolutely do. *(To Lauri)* You know?

LAURI: Oh, yeah.

PETER: Wait a second . . .

DICK: Just go on.

PETER: But where she's from affects everything *about* the story.

DICK: It's a small fix. A tiny thing, just like that. Believe me, bubbie, it's nothing. Just go on.

PETER: I don't know . . .

DICK: Go *on*. Don't worry about it. Let *us* worry about it.

PETER: Well, I had her getting pregnant when she was a junior in high school.

DENA: Oh, how awful.

PETER: Hmm?

DENA: Pregnant in high school? Isn't that like setting a really bad role model?

PETER: Well, no, I mean, realistically . . .

DENA: None of the girls at *my* high school ever would've *dreamed* . . .

DICK: Where'd you go to high school?

DENA: Holy Trinity in Green Bay? I mean, that is like a completely farfetched idea where I come from, that a girl would get herself *preg*nant . . .

PETER: Yeah, but this is Atlantic City, New Jersey, in the sixties.

DENA *(After a beat)*: Not the *six*ties.

PETER: Hmm?

DENA: I can't say I was in high school in the sixties. Are you kidding?

PETER: No?

DENA: That would put me close to forty.

PETER: Oh. Yes.

DENA: I can't play close to forty. Next you'll have me playing mothers.

*(Peter looks at Dick. A beat.)*

DICK: We'll fix it.

DENA: Something wrong?

PETER: No. I'm just a little confused. The name of the show, the title of the show, after all, is *Working MOM*.

DENA: I know. And by the way, did I tell you how much I love that title?

PETER: Yes. You did.

DENA: Well, I'm only saying: one kid, all right, I can do that. That's like an accident. Okay, I can accept that. We all make mistakes. But more than one (two or three?), I just can't see it. How many did you give her?

PETER: Well, three.

DENA: No. Now that's a stretch. We're talking about the public now, too, Peter. I have fans. They're used to seeing me on *Molly's Marauders*. I mean, that's who they think I am. There's an obligation I have. And this is very very important to me. *(To Lauri)* You're a woman, you know what I mean.

LAURI: I do, absolutely.

DENA: It's very important.

LAURI: Tell me about it.

DICK: These are all points for discussion. Let's hear what David has to say first.

PETER: Hmm?

DICK: Go 'head.

PETER: Peter.

DICK: What?

LAURI: You said "David," Dick.

DICK: No, I didn't.

DENA: Yeah, you did. I heard that, too.

*(Dena laughs, the others join her.)*

DICK: I did? Jesus, who'm I thinking of? Oh, *I* know: *him*, the schmuck. Never mind. Anyway, let's just hear what the guy has.

DENA: Yes. Let's. And by the way, I think what you've done so far is just great.

LAURI: Oh, yes.

DICK: Didn't I tell you he was something?

PETER: Anyhow . . .

DICK: He can't take a compliment. Look at him.

PETER *(Depressed)*: Well, what I had was: her high school boy-friend marries her because she's pregnant. Paulie Vanzetti his name is, or, that's what I called him. You can call him anything you like, it doesn't matter. Anyway, he never really treated her very well, so finally (this is where the pilot starts), she decides to leave him. She takes her kids— or kid, or whatever—and moves in with her mother, a kind of tart-tongued Olympia Dukakis type and—

DENA: Oh, I love that! Didn't you love her in *Moonstruck*?

LAURI: Oh, yes!

DENA: Now if this could be a kind of *Moonstruck–Fried Green Tomatoes*–fish-out-of-water–*Beverly Hills Cop* kind of thing . . .

LAURI: That's interesting. We were thinking of it more in terms of a *Moonstruck–Working Girl–Parenthood*–Tracy Chapman urban grit kind of thing.

DICK: Just think of her as a female *Rocky*.

LAURI: Yes!

DENA: I like that.

DICK: A female *Rocky*. That's all you have to say. Someone you really root for. What more is there to a good story besides rooting for someone?

DENA: I think so, too. You know? That's it, isn't it? Really really caring. God, that's so true. *(To Peter)* Please. Continue.

PETER: What's the point? I mean, we seem to be all over the place.

DICK: Uh-oh. Somebody's attitude is showing . . . *(Dena and Lauri laugh)* Look at him. He hates me. *(To Peter)* Bubbie, you gotta let go. It's the collaborative process. Everybody gets to speak his or her mind, writer or no. It's not New York theatre anymore. Now go 'head. Tell us what happens in the pilot.

PETER: Nothing. She gets a job.

DICK: Peter . . .

PETER: Okay, she gets a job working in, you know, a kind of storefront law office (they have them back east) and her boss is this old leftie attorney.

LAURI: A crusty Ed Asner–*Lou Grant*–Jerry Stiller type.

DENA: Hmm.

DICK: What?

DENA: Nothing. Well . . . What if . . . What if . . . You know what would be fun? What if she went to beauty school?

PETER: No, I don't see how that fits our idea of—

DICK: Shh.

LAURI: Sort of an urban *Steel Magnolias*.

DENA: Yes! Didn't you just love that movie?

LAURI: Oh, yes.

PETER: But I thought we were going for something gritty and socially relevant.

DICK: Who said?

DENA: Well, this way you'd get to bring in a whole lot of interesting characters. You know, the gay guy, the sassy black manicurist, the fat makeup girl? I mean, this really says something about our culture.

LAURI: You know, maybe we don't need all that backstory at all.

DENA: See, I don't think we do.

LAURI: We can get rid of the kids. We don't need the kids.

PETER: *Working Mom* without kids? Interesting.

DENA: If she's this repressed Catholic woman from Wisconsin who comes to L.A. to go to beauty school . . .

DICK: I don't hate that. I don't hate that at all.

DENA: I mean, wow, think of the possibilities, this repressed person in the middle of L.A. with all these freaks?! Talk about fish-out-of-water!

LAURI *(To Dick)*: It's a classic MTM-*Cheers*–*Murphy Brown* ensemble show. We could do three-camera, one-set (the beauty school)—

DICK: I have no problem with that—

LAURI: —and we could get it set up at NBC like that.

DENA: Oh, yes!

DICK *(To Peter)*: Maybe you should write some of this down.

PETER: And maybe *you* should go fuck yourself.

DICK: Uh-oh. There goes that attitude again.

PETER: You know, Dick? I'm sitting here thinking, What am I doing here?, I don't need this. And then I realize, Well, yeah, I do, I do need this, I need the money. And I think, That's a lousy reason to subject yourself to something like this. But *then* I think, Well, tough, you've got to survive; hell, even *Faulk*ner did this, this is what a writer has to do, just take the money and run. Okay, well *then* I ask myself, Shit, is it really worth the humiliation? Is it really worth feeling so scuzzy? Is it worth this constant burning sensation in my stomach? And the answer comes back, Yeah. It is. Just do it and stop caring about it so much. Stop thinking so much. But I *can't* stop thinking. I can't stop thinking how I could get by for two months on what it cost you guys to fly me out here. And I can't stop thinking, What is this "unique voice" shit when you won't even let me finish a sentence?

*(Peter stands and gathers his things.)*

LAURI: Peter. Please. Sit down. We can still make a go of this.

PETER *(A lover's farewell)*: No, Lauri. I'm leaving you. We're through. *(He starts to go)*

DICK: Hey.

*(Peter stops. A beat.)*

It's development, bubbie.

*(Peter goes. Pause.)*

DENA: What just happened?
DICK *(Shrugs; then)*: Typical New York writer shit.

*(Dena and Lauri nod and murmur in agreement.
Blackout.)*

# JULY 7, 1994

*This play, at long last, is for Lynn Street*

*July 7, 1994* received its premiere in March 1995 at the Humana Festival of New American Plays at Actors Theatre of Louisville (Jon Jory, Artistic Director) in Louisville, Kentucky. It was directed by Lisa Peterson. The set design was by Paul Owen, lighting was by T. J. Gerckens, sound was by Martin R. Desjardins, costumes were by Laura Patterson. The dramaturg was Michele Volansky and the stage manager was Paul Mills Holmes. The cast was as follows:

| | |
|---|---|
| KATE | Susan Knight |
| MARK | Kenneth L. Marks |
| SEÑORA SOTO | Miriam Cruz |
| MS. PIKE | Myra Lucretia Taylor |
| MR. CARIDI | Edward James Hyland |
| PAULA | Sandra Daley |

Special thanks to Lourdes Alvarez for providing the Spanish translation.

KATE, a general internist, white, thirty-nine
MARK, her husband, an academic, white, thirty-nine

KATE'S PATIENTS:

SEÑORA SOTO, Hispanic, forties
MS. PIKE, five months pregnant, black, thirties
MR. CARIDI, white, late forties
PAULA, very thin, black, thirty-six

SETTING

The play's action takes place on a single day, July 7, 1994.

The settings are the bedroom and living room of a modest house, and an examination room and waiting area in a community health clinic, both located in a small northeastern city. A television set facing away from the audience is watched by patients in the waiting area.

The play is to be performed without blackouts. As each scene ends the character from the next scene should take his or her place; the transitions should be as seamless as possible, the way a dissolve is used in film. At the start of each scene, the time of day is projected and soon fades from view.

*In the black, a slide is projected: "July 7, 1994."*
*When that slide fades out, another is projected: "6:42 A.M."*
*Kate and Mark are in bed. Kate is having a dream, whimpering in her sleep. Mark is awakened by the sounds, and gently shakes her.*

MARK: Kate? Honey?

*(Kate awakens with a slight start.)*

KATE: What.
MARK: You were dreaming.
KATE *(Still sleepy)*: Oh, yeah, I was.
MARK: Do you remember?
KATE *(Recollecting)*: I was dreaming about Matthew. Oh, God, it was terrible.
MARK: What. Tell me.
KATE: There was a flood.
MARK: Yeah? . . .
KATE: The house was flooded. There was water everywhere. It left these red water marks on the walls.
MARK: Red water marks? Are you sure it wasn't blood?
KATE: Maybe it *was* blood. Yeah, you're right, it *was* blood. And all the furniture was floating around in it, and all the books. And we were wading through it, you and I, it was kind of fun almost, we were sort of enjoying ourselves, this pool in the living room, and suddenly I got this terrible feeling: where was Matthew? We forgot about the baby! We'd left him up in the nursery! And the water, the blood, was rising, it was going up the stairs, soon the whole house was gonna be flooded, and I was trying to make it

up the stairs to get to him but the current was so strong
and I was really panic-stricken, it was awful, I thought
I wasn't going to make it up the stairs to save him.

MARK: Did you?

KATE: I don't know; you woke me up.

MARK: Sorry.

*(Pause.)*

KATE: Do you have dreams like that?, that Matthew's in distress
and you can't reach him?

MARK: Oh, all the time.

KATE: There's some encroaching catastrophe and no matter
what you do to protect him, it's no use?

MARK: Sometimes I have these morbid daydreams.

KATE: Really?

MARK: These flashes of dread that something terrible is going
to happen to him, something out of my control.

KATE: You really do? You mean it's not just me?

MARK: Oh, no, I imagine him falling down the stairs, cracking
his head open in the park, breaking free of my hand and
running into traffic . . .

KATE: What *is* it with us? We weren't always such morbid people.

MARK: We weren't parents before. Oh God, I just remembered.

KATE: What.

MARK: This dream I had the other night. I was standing, holding Matthew . . . at the Nicole Simpson murder scene.

KATE: Oh God! You're kidding.

MARK: No. We were there. Like we beamed-up on Bundy in our
pajamas. I was shielding his eyes; I didn't want him to
see. I held his face against my shoulder. But *I* could see,
very clearly, what was going on. We were invisible; I mean,
I saw us standing in that courtyard but they couldn't see
us. And it was horrifying. I mean, I saw it all, all the stuff
we saw and read about—

KATE: We have to stop watching TV. Let's get rid of the TV.

MARK *(Over "Let's get rid")*: Nicole's standing there barefoot, arguing with him, and O. J.'s completely mad, sweating, shouting . . .

KATE: You're sure it was O. J.?

MARK: Oh, yeah, and all of a sudden the knife comes out—it was very fast—and I hear it cut into her throat like, like he's slicing open a melon. *(She winces)* And I'm still clutching the baby to me hoping he won't hear or see anything. And I'm crying because I'm powerless and it's so upsetting to see. I'm watching these people lose their lives and there's nothing I can do to stop it. Their blood is trickling down the cobblestones like a creek.

*(Pause.)*

KATE: You know, maybe we really *should* think about getting rid of the TV. Look what it's doing to our dreams, it's poisoning our dreams.

MARK: I'm not getting rid of that set, we just bought that set.

KATE: Then let's shut it away somehow. Matthew's at that age when kids begin to absorb everything. I don't want him *look*ing at some of that stuff. What's it gonna do to *his* dreams?

MARK: What are you gonna do? There's nothing you can do. It's out there. It's not gonna go away. Unless you want to turn him into the "bubble boy" or something. I mean, the kid *is* gonna go to school one day, right?

*(Pause.*
*Off, Baby Matthew, announcing that he's up, calls, "Mom-ma . . . Dad-dy . . ." Mark starts to get up.)*

Well, whataya know . . . I'll go, you go back to sleep; you've got a long day.

KATE *(Over "a long day")*: No, no, I'll go, you stay . . . Stay.

*(Kate kisses him, gets out of bed and exits for the nursery. Mark pulls the covers over his head and tries to go back to sleep.*
*A slide is projected: "9:25 A.M."*
*Señora Soto, forties, sad demeanor, comes into the examination room. She takes off her blouse, hangs it up, puts on a johnny coat and, with her handbag on her lap, sits and waits. Soon, Kate enters.*
*Kate's Spanish is halting and erratic while Señora Soto's is flawless, poetic.*
*English translation appears in brackets; selected translations are projected as supertitles.)*

I'm sorry, Señora Soto, our translator, *nuestro translatora,* Loida Martinez, *¿conoces Loida Martinez?, ¿la mujer que translata aqui? (Señora shrugs)* Well, I thought she was in today but *ella es enferma hoy,* she's out sick, *no aqui,* so you're going to have to bear with me, okay? *Mi español no es muy bien,* okay? *(Señora shrugs)* So, this *dolor,* tell me about this pain. *¿Cuando dolor?* [When do you feel it?]
SEÑORA: *¿Cuando?*
KATE: *Sí.* Do you feel it . . . upon exertion? *¿Al exertione?* . . .
SEÑORA: *No comprendo.*
KATE: Sorry. *¿Tienes dificultad caminando?* [Do you have difficulty walking?] Shortness of breath? *(Señora shakes her head in apologetic uncomprehension; Kate demonstrates shortness of breath) ¿Cuantos cuadros puedes caminar?* [How many picture frames can you walk?] *(Señora is utterly confused)* Outside, *afuera,* how far *caminar antes* before you get tired? How do you say, *¿como se dice* tired? Um . . . *(She thinks)* cansado. How many blocks? *¿Cuantos cuadros?*
SEÑORA: Oh! *¡¿Cuadras?! ¡¿Cuantas cuadras?!* [Blocks? How many blocks?]
KATE: *Sí. Cuadras.*
SEÑORA *(A torrent of words): Mi vecindario es bien malo, ¿cuándo camino?* [My neighborhood is so bad, when do I walk?]

*Camino a la parada de la guagua y ruego que me dejen en
paz.* [I walk to the bus stop and pray to be left in peace.]
*Usted deberiá ver lo que está pasando en las calles.* [You
should see what's happening on the streets.] *¡Las cosas
que ocurren, debajo de nuestras narices!* [The things that go
on, right under our noses!]

KATE *(During the above)*: Señora . . . Slow . . . Slow . . .
*Despacio, por favor . . .*

SEÑORA *(Continuous)*: *Yo recuerdo cuando la gente se protegía.*
[I remember when people took care of one another.]
*Ahora nadie piensa en nada más que sí mismo.* [Now nobody
thinks about anyone but himself.] *Te matan antes de salu-
darte.* [They'd sooner kill you than say hello.]

KATE: Señora . . . *En la mañana,* in the morning, *¿si?, ¿lavantas
con dolor?* [Do you wake up with pain?]

SEÑORA: *Me despierto con dolor, me acuesto con dolor.* [I wake up
with pain, I go to sleep with pain.]

KATE: *Cuando diga "dolor," quiere decir "dolor," ¿o quiere . . . ?*
[When you say pain, do you mean pain, or do you . . . ?]

SEÑORA: *¡Quiero decir dolor! ¡Dolor! ¡Dolor!* [I mean pain!
Pain! Pain!]

KATE: Okay. The pain, *el dolor, ¿es un dolor . . .* sharp? *(Señora
shrugs; she doesn't understand)* Sharp? *¿Como un . . . cuch . . .
cuchillo?* [Like a knife?] Or heavy. . . *¿como una roca sobre
su pecho?* [Like a rock on your chest?]

SEÑORA *(Another torrent)*: *¡Me siento como que muero!* [I feel like
I'm going to die!] *¡Como que mi corazón va a explotar en mi
pecho y me voy a ahogar en mi propia sangre!* [Like my
heart is going to burst inside my chest and I'm going to
drown in my own blood!] *¿Es posible eso? ¿Puede eso
pasar, Señora doctora?* [Is that possible? Can that happen,
Doctor?]

KATE *(Over "Como que mi corazón")*: *No comprendo. Más despacio. Por favor.* Señora, slow down, *por favor. No comprendo
cuando habla tan rápido.* [I can't understand when you talk
so fast.]

SEÑORA: *Sí*. Okay. Sorry.

KATE: Let me listen to your heart, okay?, I need to *escuchar su corazón*. Okay? *(Señora doesn't understand; Kate indicates the stethoscope)* May I?

SEÑORA: Oh. *Sí, sí. (Kate listens to her chest, first the front, then the back)*

KATE: Okay. *Respira grande*. Big. *(Kate demonstrates; Señora complies)* Good. *Otra vez*. Good, *bueno*. Again. *Bueno. ¿Un otro respira grande?* Good. *(Listens carefully) ¿Otra vez? Bueno. Gracias. (Beat) ¿*Señora, *hay una historia de enfermedad de corazón en su familia?* [Is there a history of heart disease in your family?] *¿Problemas de corazón?*

SEÑORA *(Another torrent)*: *Mi mamá perdió una hija, una hijita.* [My mother lost a child, a little girl.] *Un ángel. Mi hermanita.* [An angel. My little sister.] *Y mi santa madre se murió en menos de un año.* [And my sainted mother died in less than a year.] *Se le partió el corazón.* [Her heart was broken.] *El dolor fué tan tremendo que su corazón no pudo aguantarlo.* [The pain was so great, her heart could not bear it.] *(She cries) ¡Extraño a mis hijos!* [I miss my children!]

KATE: *¿Qué?*

SEÑORA: *¡Mis hijos! ¡Mis hijos! ¡Extraño a mis hijos!* [My children! My children! I miss my children!]

KATE: *¿Dónde están tus hijos?* [Where are your children?]

SEÑORA: *En Puerto Rico.*

KATE: *¿Por qué son en Puerto Rico?* [Why are they in Puerto Rico?]

SEÑORA: *Los mandé a vivir con mi abuela.* [I sent them to live with my grandmother.] *Mi abuela los está creando.* [My grandmother is raising them.] *Son pobres pero estan seguros—más seguros de lo que estarían aquí.* [They're poor but they're safe—safer than they would be here.] *La cuidad no es lugar para los niños.* [The city is no place for children.]

KATE: *¿Tu esposo . . . ?* [Your husband . . . ?] *(Señora shrugs, speaking volumes) ¿Por que no regresas?* [Why don't you go back?]

SEÑORA: *¿A Puerto Rico?*

KATE: *Sí.*

SEÑORA: *No puedo.* [I can't.] *Lo poco que gano aquí es mucho más de lo que podría ganar allá.* [The little I make here is much more than I could make there.]

KATE: What do you do? *¿Qué . . . haces?*

SEÑORA: *¿Conoces el* Maritime Center? [Do you know the Maritime Center?]

KATE: *¿Sí?*

SEÑORA: *Limpio oficinas.* [I clean offices.] *Todo lo que gano se lo mando a ellos.* [Everything I make I send to them.] *Quiero que vayan a la universidad.* [I want them to go to college.] *Vivo sin nada.* [I live on nothing.] *Alguien tiene que trabajar.* [Somebody has to work.] *Mi abuela está muy vieja ahora.* [My grandmother is very old now.] *No puede trabjar.* [She can't work.] *Si yo volviera, nos moriríamos de hambre.* [If I went back we all would starve.]

KATE *(Overlapping; calming)*: Señora, Señora . . . *(Beat) Creo que está depresada.* [I think you are depressed.]

SEÑORA: *¿Comó?*

KATE: *Depresada.* Down. *Abajo, ¿no?* Sad. *¿Como se dice* "sad?" *(Thinks) Triste?*

SEÑORA: *¿Triste? Por supuesto estoy triste. Estoy muy triste. Mi vida es triste.* [Sad? Of course I'm sad. I'm very sad. My life is sad.] *¿Por qué no estaría triste?* [Why shouldn't I be sad?] *No sería humana si no estuviera triste.* [I wouldn't be human if I weren't sad.] *Sería un animal. Un perro. Un perro en la calle.* [I would be an animal. A dog. A dog in the streets.]

KATE: Señora, I can give you a drug . . . *Te puedo dar una medicina para . . . animar tus espíritus.* [I can give you a medicine to raise your ghosts.]

SEÑORA *(Confused)*: *¡¿Para que?!*

KATE: To raise your spirits. *Una medicina para hacerte menos triste.* [A medicine to make you less sad.] *Para elevar tu . . .* mood. A mood elevator. *¿Comprende? Para hacerte contenta.* [To make you happy.]

SEÑORA: *¿Una droga para que sea contenta?* [A drug to make me happy?]

KATE: *Sí.*

SEÑORA: *¿Una píldora?* [A pill?]

KATE: *Sí.*

SEÑORA: *¿Para qué? ¿Por qué tomaría una píldora para estar contenta?* [For what? Why would I take a pill to make me happy?] *¿Me sanaría el corazón?* [Would it heal my heart?] *Mi corazón está deshecho con razón.* [My heart is broken for a reason.] *¿Porqué voy a querer olvidarme, el porqué está deshecho mi corazón?* [Why would I want to forget why my heart is broken?]

KATE *(Overlapping)*: Señora, *estoy tratando de ayudarle.* [I'm trying to help you.]

SEÑORA *(Continuous)*: *Mi corazón está herido. Tengo el corazón herido.* [My heart is broken. I have a broken heart.]

KATE: I'm trying to help you, *ayudarle,* to offer some sort of solution.

SEÑORA *(Continuous)*: *¡Tengo dolor, Señora doctora!* [I have pain, Doctor!]

KATE: *¿Quiere ir al hospital?* [Do you want to go to the hospital?]

SEÑORA: *¡¿Hospital?!* No, no, *ningún hospital.*

KATE *(Continuous)*: *¿Quiere ir al* emergency room?

SEÑORA: *No, no* emergency room.

KATE: Señora, if you go to the hospital, they can do a stress test, *un stress test.*

SEÑORA: *Nada de hospital . . . (Makes ad-libbed rambling protestations during the following)*

KATE: Señora, I think you may be depressed. *¿Comprende?* Señora? Señora, I think you, I think it's possible depression is causing your symptoms but I'm not sure. *Pueden hacer un test para ver cómo responde su corazón al* stress. [They can give you a test to see how your heart responds to stress.]

SEÑORA *(Overlapping)*: *No, no . . .*

KATE: Then what do you want? What can I do? *(Refers to her chart)* Señora, *veo que* Dr. Leventhal *referió tú a la Clínica Hispánica para* counseling *para depresión.* [I see Dr. Leventhal referred you to the Clinica Hispanica for counseling for depression.] *¿Fué a la consultación?* [Did you go for a consultation?]

SEÑORA: *No estoy loca.* [I'm not crazy.]

KATE: Nobody said you were crazy.

SEÑORA *(Continuous)*: *Mi vida es una miseria.* [My life is miserable.] *¿Es extraño que tenga un dolor en el corazón?* [Is it any wonder I have a pain in my heart?] *Mire a mi vida.* [Look at my life.] *Mire lo que he perdido.* [Look at what I've lost.] *Mire lo que he tenido que sacrificar.* [Look at what I've had to give up.] *Mire cuán duro trabajo por unos centavos, para nada.* [Look at how hard I work for pennies, for nothing.] *Mire a mi vida.* [Look at my life.] *No necesito un psiquiatra para decirme que mi vida es dura.* [I don't need a psychiatrist to tell me my life is hard.] *Lo sé.* [I know.]

KATE: Señora, *es muy importante.* You need to follow up on your appointment at the *Clínica Hispánica.* Okay? I think the psychiatrist can help you. I am not a psychiatrist. *Es muy importante.* Okay? But if the pain comes back, *si el dolor regresa,* I mean very strong, *muy fuerte, ¿llamas la clinica?* [Will you call us here at the clinic?]

SEÑORA *(Shrugs)*: *Lo que usted quiera.* [Whatever you want.]

KATE: It's not what *I* want, it's what you need to do.

SEÑORA: *Sí, sí.*

KATE: Señora, I'm sorry . . . *Tengo que ver otros pacientes ahora.* [I'm going to have to see other patients now.] I'm very sorry. I hope you're feeling better.

*(Señora nods, turns away from Kate, silently removes the johnny coat, puts her shirt back on. As she goes:)*

I'm sorry.

*(A slide is projected: "12:08 P.M."*
*Kate is now removing stitches from the palm of a woman's*
*hand. Ms. Pike is black, in her thirties, five months pregnant.)*

MS. PIKE: Oww!

KATE: Sorry. *(Ms. Pike groans in pain)* I'm trying not to hurt
you, I'm sorry.

MS. PIKE: How many more you got?

KATE: Just a few. *(Pause) What* happened exactly?

MS. PIKE: Hmm?

KATE: *How'd* you hurt your hand?

MS. PIKE: I told you, I don't know, I cut it.

KATE: How?

MS. PIKE: Kitchen.

KATE: Yeah, I know, how?

MS. PIKE: Accident. *You* know. Damn! Could you not hurt me
so much?

KATE: I'm sorry.

MS. PIKE: This gonna take long? 'Cause I got to pick up my
daughter.

KATE: I just need to dress it; there's some infection. *(Silence*
*while she attends to her)* So, have you been following this
O. J. thing?

MS. PIKE: Oh, yeah, are you kidding? There's nothing else on.
Day and night. I'm really getting sick of it, too: O. J., O. J.,
O. J. . . . .

KATE: So what do you think?

MS. PIKE: What do I think?, you mean did he do it?

KATE: Yeah, do you think he did it?

MS. PIKE: Nah, I think it's all a frame-up.

KATE: You do? Really?

MS. PIKE: Oh, yeah. You can be sure, a famous *white* man, they
find *his* wife dead, they ain't gonna be all over *him.*

KATE: Oh, I don't know, a history of abuse?, I'm sure the ex-hus-
band is the first one they look for, no matter who he is.

MS. PIKE *(Over "who he is")*: Did anybody see him do it?

KATE: Well . . .

MS. PIKE *(Continuous)*: Did anybody *see* him? No. How do you know it wasn't some mugger who did it? Hmm? How do you know it wasn't someone out to *get* O. J.? You don't know that and neither do I. It could've been some Charles Manson thing. You don't know.

KATE: Do you think the judge is going to allow that evidence?

MS. PIKE: She better not.

KATE: Why?!

MS. PIKE: It's illegal! The cops broke the law when they hopped the wall! They had no right!

KATE: Don't you think they had just cause for entering the premises? The Bronco was on the street.

MS. PIKE *(Over "The Bronco")*: They didn't have a warrant! They had no warrant! They can't just break into somebody's house . . .

KATE: But the circumstantial evidence is pretty overwhelming, don't you think? I mean, don't you think there's sufficient cause for him to stand trial?

MS. PIKE: Those L.A. cops, they just want to get themselves one more nigger.

KATE: Why would they want to get O. J. Simpson?

MS. PIKE: Why?! *Why?!* Honey, what country do *you* live in?

*(Beat.)*

KATE: But I think you're confusing the issue; the issue is not about race.

MS. PIKE: Not about race? Sure it's about race. Everything's about race. *This* is about race. *(Meaning their exchange)*

*(Beat.)*

KATE: Maybe I'm hopelessly naive.

MS. PIKE: Maybe you are. Maybe you are. *(Beat)* I don't know, all I know is, if he *did* do it, if he *did*, you can be sure she pushed him.

KATE: Pushed him?, how do you mean?

MS. PIKE: *Pushed* him. I bet she got him so mad . . . her with her sexy clothes, waving her titties around, hanging out with those pretty boy models. I bet she got him plenty mad with her ways.

KATE: What ways?

MS. PIKE: Screwing around. She screwed everything in sight, that girl.

KATE: How do you know?

MS. PIKE: She was a tramp. That's what they say.

KATE: Who says?

MS. PIKE: All the papers. That's what you read. She drove him crazy with jealousy. That was her hold on him. I know women like this. That's how they keep their men. My sister is like this.

KATE: But she was trying to break away. She was finally on her own. It's classic, you know, when battered women—

MS. PIKE: Who said she was battered? You don't know. How do you know that? You don't know what goes on in the privacy of their own home.

KATE *(Continuous, over the above)*: —break away, when they finally break away, that's when their husbands lose it, that's when they get killed. The cops were called to their house on several occasions, she said she was afraid he was going to kill her.

MS. PIKE: Yeah?, if she was so afraid, she should've gotten the hell out of town.

KATE: Oh, come on—

MS. PIKE: She should've moved.

KATE *(Continuous, over the above)*: —take her kids out of school, away from their family and friends? He would've tracked her down anywhere.

MS. PIKE: Ah, she was too busy spending his money to leave. Too busy shopping Beverly Hills.

KATE: Did you hear that 911 tape?

MS. PIKE: Yeah, I heard it.

KATE: And? What did you think about that?

MS. PIKE: What do I think? I think they had a fight. So what? Lots of folks have fights. Doesn't mean he killed her.

KATE: Yeah, but you heard it. That was rage, pure and simple. She was terrified.

MS. PIKE: I heard the reason he was so mad? He walked in on her and some guy going down on him in the living room.

KATE: Where'd you hear that?

MS. PIKE: Waiting in line Stop 'n' Shop, one of those papers. They got sound experts to pick up what he's yelling in the background? He was yelling about her and this guy Keith.

KATE: Who's Keith?

MS. PIKE *(Shrugs)*: Some guy she was cheating with.

KATE: Wait a second, they were already divorced. She was his ex-wife, she could have sex with whomever she liked. That's not cheating. She was a single woman. And what if she *did* have sex with these guys? Does that mean she deserved to be bludgeoned to death because she was promiscuous? *(Ms. Pike makes a scoffing sound; beat)* What are you saying? She deserved it? *(Silence)*

MS. PIKE: All I'm saying . . . O. J. had no business marrying her in the first place. *If* you know what I mean. *(Silence)*

KATE: When your boyfriend hits *you*, do *you* deserve it?

MS. PIKE: What?! Who said my boyfriend hits me?

*(Kate looks at her as if to say, You can level with me. Long pause.)*

It's not the same.

KATE: Why not?

MS. PIKE: Oh, man . . .

KATE: Why isn't it?

MS. PIKE: 'Cause it's not, okay? *(Beat)* We got into a fight about the kids, that's all.

KATE: What about the kids?

MS. PIKE: I don't know, he started yelling at them about something. I got worried.

KATE: What were you worried about?

MS. PIKE: I was worried he might hit them.

KATE: Why was he yelling at them?

MS. PIKE: What are all these questions?! They were bad, okay?

KATE: Uh-huh. What were they doing that was so bad?

MS. PIKE: Yelling and screaming and stuff. You know. Talking back.

KATE: Does he hit the kids? I mean, generally?

MS. PIKE: Sometimes.

KATE: Does he hit them hard?

MS. PIKE: Sometimes he'll smack them around, yeah.

KATE: What do you mean by smack them around?

MS. PIKE: Smack them around, *you* know.

KATE: Does he smack them? Or punch them?

MS. PIKE: Yeah, smack them, punch them. Just to scare them, you know?

KATE: Uh-huh. And does he?

MS. PIKE: Oh yeah! Sometimes, he'll, *you* know, *use* things.

KATE: Use things? What do you mean?

MS. PIKE: Throw things. *You* know, plates, stuff, whatever's there. Once he threw the cat at my son.

KATE: The cat?!

MS. PIKE *(Continuous)*: Didn't like the way he talked to him?, picked up the cat?, right across the room. I couldn't believe it. You should've seen: scratches all over his face and stuff.

KATE: Sounds pretty bad.

MS. PIKE *(Shrugs)*: He got the message, though, my son.

KATE: I don't know . . . Seems to me there are other ways of getting the message across.

MS. PIKE: You got to do *some*thing. I mean, when he hits them, they deserve it. Oh, man, they deserve it alright.

KATE: Why do they deserve it?

MS. PIKE: They're out of control. You should see. They are out of control. They need discipline. They need it. My father did it. Otherwise, you know how kids get, they walk all over you. Somebody's got to take control, show them who's the boss.

KATE: So you were worried he was going to hit the kids, but you say they deserved it? I don't get it.

MS. PIKE *(Over "get it")*: I was worried he'd get carried away. *You* know.

KATE: Are they his kids?

MS. PIKE: No, no. *This* one's his, though. *(Meaning her pregnancy)*

KATE: I see. *(Beat)* So, you got into a fight over the kids, he picked up a knife, started waving it around, and you got cut.

MS. PIKE: It was an accident. He didn't mean it.

KATE: No, you just happened to walk into it.

MS. PIKE: He was mad. He just wanted to scare me.

KATE: "Scare" you? Does he hit you a lot?

MS. PIKE: No! Not a lot. Sometimes. Sometimes he'll, you know, give me a punch I do something he don't like.

KATE: Like what? What could you possibly do to warrant a punch?

MS. PIKE *(Over "to warrant a punch")*: Could be anything. What I cooked, what I say. He don't like it when I talk back.

KATE: That sounds pretty difficult. *(Ms. Pike shrugs)* I mean, you never know when you might set him off.

MS. PIKE: Oh, I have a pretty good idea.

KATE: He just went after you with a knife!

MS. PIKE *(Shrugs)*: Yeah, well . . . I interfered—

KATE: You what?!

MS. PIKE *(Continuous)*: —I shouldn't've.

KATE: Is that what he told you?

MS. PIKE: No, it's the truth. I should've butt out. It was none of my business. He had words with the kids, I should've butt out.

KATE *(Over "I should've butt out")*: They're your children! Ms. Pike! This man is abusing you and your children!

MS. PIKE: What, you're gonna lecture me now?

KATE: Why would you, why would *any*one deserve to be hit?

MS. PIKE: In his eyes I do.

KATE: I'm not talking about his eyes.

MS. PIKE: I mean, the way he sees it, I do something pisses him off—wham.

KATE: Yeah, but do you feel you deserve it?

MS. PIKE: I'm used to it by now.

KATE: That's not what I'm asking.

MS. PIKE: It's the way it is. If that's the way it has to be . . .

KATE: It doesn't have to be that way, there are people you can talk to, you know, agencies.

MS. PIKE *(Over "agencies")*: Shit . . .

KATE *(Continuous)*: I can walk you over to meet someone right here at the clinic, I can introduce you to someone right now.

MS. PIKE *(Over "right now")*: What, so they'd tell me to leave him? Tell me to walk out on him? *Then* what? Then what happens to me? What happens to my kids? Look, lady, you don't know *me*. You don't know a *damn* thing about my life.

KATE: True enough.

MS. PIKE: I came for you to take out my stitches.

*(Kate nods. A beat. While writing a prescription, back to business:)*

KATE: Here's an antibiotic for that infection. Three times a day for ten days with meals. And try to keep that hand dry.

*(Kate rips the prescription off the pad, hands it to her.
A slide is projected: "3:53 P.M."
Kate is with Mr. Caridi, an unstable, working-class man in his late forties.)*

What brings you here today, Mr. Caridi?

MR. CARIDI: You. *(Kate good-naturedly rolls her eyes)* No, I mean it, I been thinking about you. I have; that's the truth.

KATE *(Over "that's the truth"; keeping her professional cool)*: Mr. Caridi, do you have a complaint?

MR. CARIDI: Only that I don't see you enough. *(Another disapproving look from Kate; she is not charmed)* What's the matter, I'm embarrassing you? A beautiful girl like you? *Look* at you, you're blushing.

KATE: I am not.

MR. CARIDI: Don't you know you're beautiful?

KATE: Come on, this is really . . .

MR. CARIDI *(Over "this is really")*: Doesn't your husband tell you how beautiful you are? Boy, if you were mine, if you were *mine*, I'd tell you all the *time*, all the *time* I'd tell you.

KATE *(Over "all the time I'd tell you")*: Mr. Caridi, do you have any idea how inappropriate this is? No, honestly. Do you? I'm your *doctor*, Mr. Caridi.

MR. CARIDI: Hey . . . *(Meaning, "You don't have to tell me")*

KATE *(Continuous)*: Do you think you can respect that fact for ten minutes so that I can do my job?

MR. CARIDI: Shoot.

KATE: Thank you.

*(Beat.)*

MR. CARIDI: Can I say one thing, though? You know?, in the beginning I really thought I was gonna have a problem having a lady doctor. But, no, I like it. I really do.

KATE: That's good, Mr. Caridi. I'm glad.

MR. CARIDI: There's something really nice about it, you know? Really refreshing.

KATE: Would you like to tell me what's wrong?

MR. CARIDI *(Dead serious)*: I really have been thinking about you, you know. I missed you.

KATE: Mr. Caridi, this has got to stop. Okay? Because if you insist on this inappropriate behavior—

MR. CARIDI: Don't get so worked up!

KATE: —I'm going to have to take you off my patient list and give you to Dr. Leventhal. Do you understand?

MR. CARIDI: Yes, Teacher—I mean, Doctor. *(He cracks himself up; she glares at him)* That was a joke! Come on! Where's your sense of humor?

KATE: Mr. Caridi, is there a medical reason that brought you here today?

MR. CARIDI: Yeah. What do you think, I make appointments just to see you? *(She says nothing)* I'm missing O. J. for this! Today's the big day!

KATE: Mr. Caridi, I'm already running twenty minutes late.

MR. CARIDI: Okay, okay, I see you're into being super-serious. I can be super-serious, too. *(He folds his hands like a student)*

KATE: Well?

MR. CARIDI: I got a few things I care to discuss.

KATE: All right.

MR. CARIDI: Some personal matters.

KATE: Personal matters or health problems?

MR. CARIDI: Yeah. Health problems. *(Pause)* You still want me to give up smoking?

KATE: Is that really why you're here? You want to talk about quitting smoking?

MR. CARIDI: I know, I know.

KATE *(Continuous)*: We've talked about this before.

MR. CARIDI: I try. I really do. I just can't. The minute I decide to quit, I can't wait to light up again. Believe me, I'd be so happy to come and see you and tell you I quit. I couldn't wait to see the look on your face when I told you.

KATE: Maybe it's time to think about the patch.

MR. CARIDI: The what?

KATE: The nicotine patch. Remember?

MR. CARIDI *(Shakes his head no)*: What's that?

KATE: You wear it on your skin and it releases nicotine into your bloodstream. It takes away the craving.

MR. CARIDI: No kidding.

KATE: Would you like to try it?

MR. CARIDI: Yeah, sure, why not? Does it hurt?

KATE: No, you just wear it on your skin. Like a Band-Aid. Before you go I'll give you a starter kit. And then you'll need to fill this prescription. *(She writes)* Okay?

MR. CARIDI: Yeah, Doc. Thanks.

*(He watches her write in silence, then he refers to a framed photo:)*

That your kid?

KATE: What?

MR. CARIDI *(Points to the photo)*: The kid.

KATE: Yes.

*(Pause.)*

MR. CARIDI: Can I see?

KATE: Mr. Caridi . . .

MR. CARIDI: Can't I see the picture? I just want to see it. I don't got my glasses. Can I see it up close? I love kids.

*(Kate hesitates, but then hands him the frame.)*

Thanks.

*(He looks at the photo for a long time, which she finds terribly unnerving. Kate extends her hand.)*

KATE: Mr. Caridi?

MR. CARIDI: So: that's your kid.

KATE: Yes. *(Beat)* May I have it back, please?

MR. CARIDI: That your husband?

KATE: Yes.

MR. CARIDI: Pretty kid. What's his name?

KATE *(Hesitates)*: Matthew.

MR. CARIDI: Matthew, huh.

KATE: May I please . . . ?

MR. CARIDI: *(Still looking)* Looks like you, don't he.

KATE: Mr. Caridi, please . . . Can we get on with this? I've got a whole bunch of patients I've got to see.

*(Laughing, he taunts her with the picture frame.)*

Mr. Caridi . . . Mr. Caridi, please . . .

*(He gives Kate the photo; she puts it back. Pause.)*

MR. CARIDI: I wish I had that.

KATE: Had what?

MR. CARIDI: A kid, a family. Maybe if I had a kid . . . If I didn't have this . . . disability . . . Who knows? I might be sitting where you are. Or where your husband sits. You ever think about that? There but for the grace of God?

KATE: All the time. *(Beat)* Mr. Caridi, have you been taking your lithium?

MR. CARIDI: Why?

KATE: I suspect you haven't.

*(Beat.)*

MR. CARIDI: No.

KATE: Why not?

MR. CARIDI *(Shrugs)*: I hate the way it makes me feel. Makes my mouth taste like shit.

KATE: You can always use a mouthwash if it dries out your mouth. Or chew gum. Mr. Caridi, you've got to be sure to tell your psychiatrist—when's your next appointment? *(He shrugs)* Have you been going to your appointments?

MR. CARIDI: I don't like him. Why can't I see you?

KATE: I'm not a psychiatrist. Mr. Caridi, you've got to take your lithium and you've got to take it regularly, do you understand? You have bipolar disease—

MR. CARIDI: Yeah yeah yeah.

KATE *(Continuous)*: —it's a disease, controllable by drugs.

MR. CARIDI *(Shrugs)*: I got another problem I got to ask you.

KATE: What kind of problem?

MR. CARIDI: It's kind of personal.

KATE *(Beat)*: All right.

MR. CARIDI: Kind of confidential. *(She nods okay)* You're my doctor, right?

KATE: Yes.

MR. CARIDI: I can discuss a personal problem with you, can't I? I mean, that's appropriate, isn't it? Hmm? Doctor-patient thing? Like confession, right?

KATE: What's the problem, Mr. Caridi?

*(Pause.)*

MR. CARIDI: It's my penis.

*(Beat.)*

KATE: Yes?

MR. CARIDI: I don't know, something don't seem right.

KATE: Can you be more specific?

MR. CARIDI: Sometimes . . . Sometimes I have this burning sensation.

KATE: It's painful when you urinate?

MR. CARIDI: I don't know, I think so. Yeah, it is. And sometimes it gets really big and red and swollen; I think you better take a look, Doc. *(He starts to undo his pants)*

KATE: All right, all right, that's it!

MR. CARIDI *(Feigning shock)*: What!

KATE: I did not tell you to take your pants down. *(His pants fall to his feet)*

MR. CARIDI: Don't you want to see what's the matter?!

KATE: Mr. Caridi . . .

227

MR. CARIDI *(Continuous)*: I tell you I got something wrong with my penis, don't you think you'd better take a look?! What's the matter, you shy? You're a doctor!, you've seen naked men before.

KATE *(Over "naked men before")*: That's right, I'm not your friend, I'm not your girlfriend, I'm your doctor. Now put your pants back on before I call for help.

MR. CARIDI *(His pants still around his ankles)*: How do you know there isn't something really wrong with me?!

KATE: You're right, I don't.

MR. CARIDI *(Continuous)*: How do you know I don't have cancer or a tumor or something?

KATE: Mr. Caridi, pull up your pants, Mr. Caridi . . .

MR. CARIDI *(Continuous)*: What kind of doctor are you? Aren't you supposed to heal the sick? Aren't you?! You and Hillary Clinton! Phony bitches! All smiles and promises.

KATE *(Overlapping)*: I'm setting up another appointment for you with Dr. Leventhal.

MR. CARIDI: What?! Why?!

KATE *(Continuous)*: I think Dr. Leventhal should be your primary care physician from now on. I think you need to see a male physician.

MR. CARIDI: Oh, come on! What kind of shit is this? What kind of doctor are you, anyway? You're no doctor. Where's your compassion? Doctors are supposed to have compassion.

KATE: Excuse me, I'll go get that patch.

*(Kate leaves.)*

MR. CARIDI: Bitch.

*(Pause. He picks up the picture frame to look at again, then impulsively hides it in his newspaper. She returns with the patch.)*

KATE: Here, let me show you, all you do is . . .

*(He snatches the patch from her. As he goes:)*

MR. CARIDI: Suck my dick.

*(A slide is projected: "6:10 P.M."*
  *Kate is with a woman, Paula, black, thirty-six, frail and sick.)*

PAULA: "Mama, I want to see Lion King! I want to *see Lion King*!" I mean, that's all I've been hearing for weeks. "Why can't I see it? Why can't I see it?" You go to *Bur*ger King, everything is *Lion King*. You go to the store . . .

KATE: How old is she again?

PAULA: Four and a half, be five in October.

KATE: That's what I thought; that's a little young.

PAULA: Right? I mean, isn't that what everybody's saying? "Well, Kaisha's mother let her see it. Trevor's mother let him see it." Well, I was getting real sick and tired hearing whose mother let who see it—I mean, that's all this girl talked about! Day in, day out. I told her, "Lookit, your brother saw it and your sister saw it and they both say you're too young, so forget about it, you're not seeing it, I don't want to hear another word!" Well. To make a long story short . . . yesterday I get my girlfriend Clarisse drop us off at Showcase in Orange—

KATE: You pushover!

PAULA *(Continuous)*: —and I take Alexandra to *Lion King*. Yeah.

KATE: And?

PAULA: You see it? *(Kate shakes her head)* How old's your boy?

KATE: Just over two.

PAULA: Oh. Well. I don't know who was more upset by it, her or me. You know what happens in it?

KATE: I think so.

PAULA: The father lion dies and Scar makes Simba think it's all his fault?

229

KATE: Uh-huh.

PAULA: Man. Pretty heavy stuff. Well, I'm not sure it was such a great idea. Maybe it was, maybe it wasn't. All I know is, the father dies, right?, and I'm holding my little girl to me, and I'm sobbing my eyes out.

KATE: Oh, Paula . . .

PAULA: And I mean *sob*bing. Like the dams burst. Whooshh! I totally lose it. I don't know what freaked her out more, me or the stampede. And it's so noisy! It's so loud! It's really scary, it really is, I don't care *what* they say. And I can't stop crying! It's like uncontrollable. Like everything in my life, all the shit, all the disease, everything, is pouring out of my eyes in tears. A flood!, this flood is . . . And grownups are looking at me funny like, What the fuck *she* on? And kids are getting freaked-out all around us—"Mommy, who's that crazy lady?"—and I'm squeezing little Alexandra to me and squeezing her and squeezing her with all my might and wailing and rocking and making an all-around *fool* of myself.

KATE *(Soothingly)*: No . . .

PAULA *(Continuous)*: And then, all of a sudden, it stops. Just like that. Like somebody turned off the water, turned off the faucet, you know? And I'm sitting there, so wrecked, so wasted . . . And it's just a stupid cartoon! A kids' movie! I don't know what the hell set me off like that. Man! *(Long pause)*

KATE: Paula . . . *(Pause)* The DDI isn't working.

PAULA: Did I tell you?, at the movies?, she had me getting up for *pop*corn, getting up for *Sprite*, getting up to *pee* . . .

KATE: Paula?

*(Beat.)*

PAULA: So put me back on AZT.

KATE: We can't put you back on AZT.

PAULA *(Over "on AZT")*: Why not?

KATE: It doesn't work that way. It stopped being effective the first time, it's not going to be effective now.

PAULA *(Over "effective now")*: How do you know?

KATE: It isn't. *(Beat)* The sputum and blood cultures we took? Both grew out *M. avium intracellulare*.

PAULA: M. what?

KATE: *M. avium intracellulare*. It's a mycobacterium, a kind of a cousin of TB. That's one of the reasons you haven't been able to keep the weight back on.

PAULA: That last pneumonia took a long time, too. Remember? I was sick forever—

KATE: This isn't like that.

PAULA *(Continuous)*: —and I pulled through.

KATE: Yeah, but it's not the same. You were stronger then. You had more resistance. *(Pause)* Paula, your T-4 count is down to four. Four. That's as low as it goes; it can't *get* any lower than that. *(Pause)* Paula . . . With your T-cell count so low . . .

PAULA *(Drops eye contact)*: Yeah? . . .

KATE: Anything can happen. And it will.

PAULA: Uh-huh.

*(Beat.)*

KATE: Paula?

PAULA *(Gets up)*: Lookit, I got to go pick up my kids at my mother. I'm late, I told her I'd get there at six.

KATE: Paula, please sit down?

PAULA *(Over "sit down"; enraged)*: You kept me waiting twenty minutes out there!—

KATE: Paula . . .

PAULA *(Continuous)*: —My time is valuable, too, you know. May not look it to you . . .

KATE: Please.

*(Pause. Paula leans against the chair.)*

*(Carefully)* I think it's time to give some serious thought
... Remember we talked about this? I think it's time to
come up with a plan. *(Beat)* Did you meet with the social
worker?

PAULA: Yeah.

KATE: And?

PAULA *(Shrugs)*: Her perfume made me sick to my stomach.

KATE: Paula, I know it's hard.

PAULA: You don't know shit. You don't know nothing. When
was the last time *you* had to worry what was gonna happen to *your* kids? So don't tell me you know.

*(Kate nods. Long pause.)*

KATE: What did your mother say?

PAULA: My mother don't want them. Can you blame her? I don't.
My mother is fifty-four years old. What does she want a
bunch of kids for? She's tired. She's got diabetes, bad cir-
culation. High blood pressure—

KATE: I know.

PAULA *(Continuous)*: —I mean, a couple of days here and there,
when I'm in the hospital or whatever, *that* she can handle.
But raising kids that ain't even teenagers yet?! Un-uh.
She's done. She's had it. And can you *blame* her with
what's going on today? Who needs it? She's tired. She
raised kids her whole life. Her kids, my sister's kids. My
little one? André? He's a devil. She can't go chasing him
around. How she gonna do that? She can't.

KATE: But they're your *chil*dren. Her *grand*children.

PAULA: You don't understand: she don't want no more children. You understand? She don't *want* them.

KATE: Would she come to a family meeting?

PAULA: I'm telling you she don't want them. Period.

KATE *(Over "Period")*: If I arranged a family meeting, if I called
her and talked to her myself ...

PAULA: You don't get it, do you. Forget about my mother. Forget about her. Make believe she's dead. Make believe I don't *have* a mother. 'Cause she ain't gonna take them.

KATE: All I'm asking is, Paula, can you get her down here for a meeting, that's all I'm asking. *(Paula shrugs)* You, me, the social worker, your mother, maybe your girlfriend . . .

PAULA: Clarisse?

KATE: Yeah, have you considered *her*?

PAULA: Clarisse has got four kids of her own! No man, no job, no money, no nothing. How'm I gonna leave my four kids on her doorstep?

KATE: Isn't there somebody else, a friend or a . . .

PAULA: *All* my friends got problems of their own. Who do you think my friends are? Rich folks? How my friends gonna raise my kids? I can't ask them that. They got problems feeding them*selves.*

KATE: Paula, what I'm concerned about right now are your *child*ren, what's going to happen to your *child*ren.

PAULA: And you think I'm not?

KATE: Of course I don't think that. I'm just trying to—

PAULA: I bet you're sitting there asking yourself what business did she have having all these kids for in the first place?

KATE: No . . .

PAULA: Well, I had no business doing a lot of the things I did. But the thing is I did 'em. Okay? And this is where we're at. *(Pause)* You just think I'm selfish.

KATE: I never said that.

PAULA: You do. You think I'm too selfish to think about my kids.

KATE: That's not true. I just think there's no time to fool around.

PAULA: Fool a*round*?! It look to you like I'm fooling around?

KATE *(Over "like I'm fooling around"; overly invested)*: You know what I'm saying. This is no time to be passive, Paula, there's no time for that. You *need* a plan. Think about your children. Losing you is going to be hard enough, what if they all get separated from each *oth*er? Hmm?

Have you thought about that? They'll be shipped all over the place and get tossed around in the child welfare system and maybe get lost forever. Is that what you want for them? You can't let that happen to them, Paula. You've got to plan for it now. Before you get any sicker.

PAULA: You just want to see me dead.

KATE: What?!

PAULA: It's true. You'll be happy when I'm out of your hair forever.

KATE: How can you say that? I've followed you for two and a half years. I care very much about you.

PAULA *(Over "about you")*: Nah, I'm too much trouble. You'll be happy when I just disappear. One day I will, too, I'll just . . . poof! and that'll be it. "'Bye, 'bye, Paula. Oh, well, too bad. Next!"

KATE: Paula, let me talk to your mother?

*(Pause.)*

PAULA: Look at me. Look at where I'm at. *(She shakes her head)* My whole life. My whole fucking life: men. Bad luck with men. Lamar should've just slashed my throat. It've been easier, a lot easier than this, that's for sure. A quick knife to the jugular? Sounds good. Sounds good to me. *(Beat)* Know what it's gonna say on my tombstone? FUCKED OVER BY MEN. My daddy fucked me over, Lamar finished me off. *(Beat)* I'm thirty-six years old. Can you believe it? Look at this body, this saggy bag of bones. I look a *hun*dred and thirty-six.

KATE: No . . .

PAULA: This body used to mean something.

KATE: It still does.

PAULA *(Shakes her head; then)*: No. No. It was a good body, once. It had value. Now? *(Pause)* I think back to meeting Lamar? First laying eyes on him? And I think to myself, Stay away, girl, this man is going to ruin you. This man will make your life hell. This man will poison you and the two of you'll die young and your children'll be cursed forever. *(Beat)* Did I know, deep down, I was meeting Death himself? Is that what attracted me to him? Did Nicole know when she first laid eyes on that beautiful man? Did she know O. J. was Death and go to him anyway? If Lamar was Death, then let me tell you: Death was hot.

*(Kate smiles sadly. She puts her hand in Paula's. Paula doesn't reject it.*
*A slide is projected: "9:12 P.M."*
*Kate finishes writing notes on a chart and packs up for the night. She looks at the framed photos and sees that her picture is gone. She realizes that it was swiped by Mr. Caridi.)*

KATE: Sonofabitch.

*(Señora Soto appears at the door.)*

SEÑORA: *¿Señora doctora?*
KATE: Oh, hello.
SEÑORA: *Dijo que la llamara. Llamé y me dijeron que podia venir.* [You said to call. I called, they said I could come in.]
KATE: *Sí, sí. Entra. Me voy a casa.* I'm going home, *terminé por la noche.* [Finished for the night.] *Sólo puedo ver usted por un minuto.* [I can only see you for a minute.] *¿Que pasó?* [What happened?]
SEÑORA: *Sentí el dolor otra vez. Volvió el dolor.* [I felt the pain again. The pain came back.] *Dijo que deberia llamar si sentia otra vez el dolor.* [You said I should call if I felt the pain.]
KATE: *Sí. ¿Cuándo paso?* [When did it happen?]
SEÑORA: *Estaba descansador en mi "Lazy Boy."* [I was resting in my Lazy Boy recliner chair.] *Estaba viendo a O. J. Simpson.* [I was watching O. J. Simpson.] *De pronto, me vino una visión.* [Then all of a sudden I had a vision.]

KATE: *¿Una visión?*

SEÑORA: *Sí. Mi corazón empezó a latir fuertemente en mi pecho.* [My heart began to pound in my chest.] *La sangre empezó a correr de mi boca—* [Blood started pouring out of my mouth— ] *como un río de sangre—* [like a river of blood—] *y de los ojos, y de los oidos y la nariz.* [and out of my eyes, and my ears and my nose.] *La sangre corrio de mi—* [Blood gushed out of me—] *de alla debajo, de todas partes—* [from down there, from everywhere—] *llenando el cuarto de sangre.* [filling the room with blood.] *Mi sangre estaba por todo, como un mar.* [My blood was everywhere, like the sea.] *Y pronto los muebles empezaron a bambolear en la sangre—* [Soon the furniture started bobbing around in the blood—] *el televisor, las sillas, y pronto todo flotó por la ventana.* [the TV, the chairs, and soon everything floated right out the window.] *¡Y yo oía a mis hijos llorando!* [And I heard my children crying!] *¡Ellos estaban en algun otro cuarto, llorando, "¡Mamá! ¡Mamá!"* [They were in another room somewhere, crying, "Mama! Mama!"] *Yo no los oía pero si los veía.* [I could hear them but I couldn't see them.] *¡Yo no podía llegar hacia ellos!* [I couldn't get to them!] *La olas de sangre eran tan grandes.* [The waves of blood were so strong.] *Que me barraron como una terrible tormenta.* [It tossed me around like a terrible storm.] *¡Y no podía nadar! ¡Me ahogué!* [And I couldn't swim! The waves overtook me and I drowned!] *¡Me ahogué en mi propia sangre!* [Drowned in my own blood!] *Señora doctora, ¿puede que el dolor haga que se explote el corazón de una madre?* [Can sorrow make a mother's heart burst open?] *¿Se puede ahogar uno en su propia sangre?* [Can you drown in your own blood?] *Creo que es posible.* [I think it's possible.] *¡Creo que voy a morir!* [I think I'm going to die!] *¡Por favor, no quiero que me lleven de mis hijos!* [Please, I don't want to be taken from my children!]

KATE *(Soothing)*: Señora . . .

SEÑORA: *Ya no puede dormir.* [I can't sleep anymore.] *Tengo conversaciones en mi mente con mis hijos.* [I have conversations in my head with my children.] *Les hablo toda la noche.* [I talk to them all night.] *Pienso en ellos todo el día.* [I think about them all day.] *Pienso en ellos ahora mismo.* [I'm thinking about them now.] *Me duele el corazón.* [My heart aches.] *¡Creo que voy a morir!* [I think I am going to die!] *¡El dolor! ¡El dolor!* [The pain! The pain!]

KATE: *El dolor es miedo.* [The pain is fear.]

SEÑORA: *¿Qué?*

KATE: *El dolor es miedo.* Fear. *Tienes miedo.* [The pain is fear. You're afraid.]

SEÑORA: *Sí, tengo miedo. Estoy tan asustada.* [Yes, I am afraid. I'm so afraid.] *¿Señora doctora, ¿que voy a hacer?* [What am I going to do?] *Ayúdame, Señora doctora. Ayúdame.* [Help me, Doctor. Help me.]

*(Kate and Señora stand at opposite ends of the room in silence.*

*A slide is projected: "10:05 P.M."*

*Mark is seated on a sofa, his bare feet up, reading the* New York Times. *Kate comes in from work.)*

KATE: Hi.

MARK: Hi. How are you?

*(Kate kisses him, shrugs. A beat. He senses something is wrong.)*

What.

KATE *(Shrugs it off)*: Baby sleeping?

MARK: Yeah. He was still flinging himself around the crib a couple of minutes ago but it's been pretty quiet.

KATE: I'm tempted to go in.

MARK *(Takes her hand to stop her)*: Don't. Please? You'll wake him.

*(Pause. She takes off her shoes and joins him on the sofa.)*

KATE: *Frasier* on?

MARK: Rerun.

KATE: Which one?

MARK: He and Niles take his father out to eat? The steakhouse?

KATE: Oh, yeah.

MARK: I turned it off.

KATE: What about *Seinfeld*?

MARK: That was a rerun, too, but I didn't remember seeing it.

KATE: What was it?

MARK: Elaine's in the ladies' room at a movie theatre? and finds there's no toilet paper and asks the woman in the stall next to hers for some and the woman refuses and they argue but can't see each other and of course it turns out the woman is Jerry's new girlfriend.

KATE: Of course . . .

MARK: And Elaine has a new boyfriend who she's very defensive about because he's supposedly so good-looking. And Kramer and George and this guy go rock climbing and somehow, I don't know exactly, I was reading the paper, I think George drops a rope or something and the guy falls and crushes his face.

KATE *(Winces)*: Oooh.

MARK: Yeah. And then naturally it turns out that Elaine was only interested in him for his looks and has no interest in staying with him if he's disfigured. And also there's this phone-sex subplot going on with Kramer, where it turns out that the woman he's been calling is Jerry's new girlfriend.

KATE: Was it any good?

MARK: It was all right. *Seinfeld*'s getting very, I don't know, there's something very malevolent going on on *Seinfeld*. Something mean-spirited and juvenile.

KATE: Uh-huh.

MARK: The attitude toward sex is very screwed-up. All this fear and loathing. The women are always portrayed as these

alien ciphers good for making out with but there's this
underlying ickiness and suspicion. All the women except
Elaine all seem to have cooties.

KATE: Mmm. Seinfeld seems like a seriously anally retentive guy.

MARK: Right! I mean, anybody who has fifteen cereal boxes
lined up like that . . . You hungry? There's some tortellini left in the fridge.

KATE *(Shakes her head no)*: What happened today?

MARK: You heard that the judge ruled that the evidence was
admissable?

KATE: I heard that; I meant what's new with you?

MARK: Not much.

KATE: Did you talk to many people today?

MARK: You mean besides a two year old and the UPS man?

KATE: That's what I thought. How's the writing coming?

MARK: Maybe I'll be done with this dissertation by the time I'm
fifty. Maybe. There's an O. J. update on NBC if you're
up for it.

KATE: I'm not.

MARK: Are you okay?

KATE *(Thinks about elaborating)*: Oh . . . *(But changes her mind)*
Tell me about our boy. What kind of a day did he have?

MARK: I hear he had a good day.

KATE: Tell me. What did you do tonight?

MARK: Well, we ate tortellini—

KATE: Yeah . . .

MARK *(Continuous)*: —which he kept popping into his mouth,
it was really quite impressive, he can really put it away.
And then we went for a walk.

KATE: Where?

MARK: The construction site and then to the park.

KATE: Oh, a serious walk.

MARK: And we saw the "backhoe" and the crane—"biigg
crane"—and we saw bicyclists and doggies and men running. It was a banner day. And an airplane flew overhead
and birdies, and later he pointed way up high in the sky—

"Look, Daddy, hec-coc-ca," and he was right, there was a helicopter. And we went and got some frozen yogurt which he ate with great abandon and got all over himself. And we ran into Pete closing up which was a source of great excitement. And then we got home and I let him play with the hose while I mowed the lawn.

KATE: You mowed? Excellent.

MARK: So he got soaked and ucky and then we went upstairs and got naked and chased each other around for a little while and he peed on the floor—deliberately—"Look, Daddy, pee!" And I got him into the tub where he peed some more and scrubbed my face with the wash cloth— very hard—I had to take it away from him.

KATE: Did you shampoo?

MARK: Not tonight; I couldn't bring myself to. I couldn't take away the wash cloth *and* wash his hair; that would've been too cruel. And then I got him ready for bed.

KATE: What did you read?

MARK: What did we read. Let's see . . . we read the bulldozer book. And the truck book. And the piggy book. And the potty book—he now says: "I want read potty book," you know, he's fascinated, we'd better go get him a potty, quick, this weekend, before the window of opportunity slams shut forever. *(Pause)* You know how it is when you turn out the light and you're holding him on your lap and you can see his dark eyes shining and you can smell his milky breath and he seems utterly content and starts getting sleepy and his eyes begin to close but he forces himself awake?

KATE: Mmm. He's an angel.

MARK: I sat like that with him in my arms for a while and I said, "In the great green room, there was a telephone, and a red balloon," and he crinkled up his face in pure pleasure.

KATE: Say it.

MARK: What.

KATE: "In the great green room . . ."

MARK: "In the great green room, there was a telephone, and a red balloon, and a picture of the cow jumping over the moon."

*(She is weeping; he becomes concerned.)*

Honey? What is it?

*(She shakes her head dismissively.)*

Bad day?

KATE: That's the thing: it was completely typical; it just got to me today.

MARK: You want to tell me?

KATE: Just finish the story.

MARK: What?

KATE: Finish. Go ahead. *(He hesitates)* Please? I want to hear your voice.

*(Beat.)*

MARK *(Recites from memory)*: "And there were three little bears sitting on chairs. And two little kittens. And a pair of mittens. And a little toyhouse. And a young mouse. And a comb and a brush and a bowl full of mush. And a quiet old lady who was whispering 'hush.'" *(Beat)* "Goodnight room. Goodnight moon. Goodnight cow jumping over the moon. Goodnight light and the red balloon. Goodnight bears. Goodnight chairs. Goodnight kittens. And goodnight mittens. Goodnight clocks. And goodnight socks." *(Pause; she is sobbing)* "Goodnight little house. And goodnight mouse. Goodnight comb. And goodnight brush. Goodnight nobody. Goodnight mush. And goodnight to the old lady whispering 'hush.' Goodnight stars. Goodnight air. Goodnight noises everywhere."

*(He holds her as lights fade.)*

241

DONALD MARGULIES received the 2000 Pulitzer Prize for Drama for *Dinner with Friends* (Variety Arts Theatre, New York; Comedie des Champs-Elysees, Paris; Actors Theatre of Louisville; South Coast Repertory). The play received numerous awards, including the American Theatre Critics Association New Play Award, Dramatists Guild/Hull-Warriner Award, Lucille Lortel Award, Outer Critics Circle Award and a Drama Desk nomination.

His many plays include *Collected Stories* (Theatre Royal Haymarket, London; South Coast Repertory; Manhattan Theatre Club; HB Studio/Lucille Lortel Theatre), which received the Los Angeles Drama Critics Circle/Ted Schmitt Award, L.A. Ovation Award, a Drama Desk nomination, and was a finalist for both the Dramatists Guild/Hull-Warriner Award and the Pulitzer Prize; *Sight Unseen* (South Coast Repertory, Manhattan Theatre Club/Orpheum Theatre), which received an OBIE Award, Dramatists Guild/Hull-Warriner Award, a Drama Desk nomination, and was also a Pulitzer Prize finalist; *The Model Apartment* (Los Angeles Theatre Center; Primary Stages, New York), which received an OBIE Award, Drama-Logue Award, a Drama Desk nomination, and was also a Dramatists Guild/Hull-Warriner Award finalist; *The Loman Family Picnic* (Manhattan Theatre Club), which received a Drama Desk nomination; *What's Wrong with This Picture?* (Manhattan Theatre Club, Jewish Repertory Theatre, Brooks Atkinson Theatre); *Broken Sleep: Three Plays* (Williamstown Theatre Festival); *July 7, 1994* (Actors Theatre of Louisville); *Found a Peanut* (The Joseph Papp Public Theater/New York Shakespeare Festival); *Pitching to the Star* (West Bank Cafe); *Resting Place* (Theater for the New City);

*Gifted Children*; *Zimmer* and *Luna Park* (the last three all receiving productions at the Jewish Repertory Theatre).

His adaptation of Sholem Asch's Yiddish classic, *God of Vengeance*, which had its world premiere at ACT Theatre in Seattle, will be presented at the Williamstown Theatre Festival in 2002. His latest play, *Brooklyn Boy*, was commissioned by South Coast Repertory.

Mr. Margulies has received grants from the National Endowment for the Arts, the New York Foundation for the Arts and the John Simon Guggenheim Memorial Foundation. He was the recipient of the 2000 Sidney Kingsley Award for Outstanding Achievement in Theatre. Mr. Margulies is an alumnus of New Dramatists and serves on the council of The Dramatists Guild of America.

His screen adaptation of *Dinner with Friends* was produced by HBO and a television production of *Collected Stories* was broadcast on PBS Hollywood Presents. He has developed screenplays for NBC, Paramount Pictures, Propaganda, Touchstone Pictures, Warner Brothers, TriStar and Universal, and has written more than twenty unproduced screenplays for a wide range of industry talent, including Alec Baldwin, Michael Douglas, Spike Lee, Bette Midler, Oliver Stone, Robin Williams and Bruce Willis.

Born in Brooklyn, New York, in 1954, Mr. Margulies currently lives with his wife Lynn Street, who is a physician, and their son Miles, in New Haven, Connecticut, where he teaches playwriting at Yale University.